D1516145

Off**Season**

Living the
retirement
dream

Other books from *The Sun*:

Marylanders Of The Century,
    edited by Barry Rascovar

Are We There Yet? Recollections Of Life's Many Journeys,
    by Elise T. Chisolm

Miss Prudence Pennypack's Perfectly Proper,
    by Karen E. Rupprecht

A Century In The Sun: Photographs Of Maryland

A Century In The Sun: Front Pages Of The Twentieth Century

A Century In The Sun: Postcards Of Maryland's Past

Dining In Baltimore: Food And Drink In And Around Charm City

Hometown Boy: The Hoodle Patrol And Other Curiosities Of Baltimore, by Rafael Alvarez

The Wild Side Of Maryland, An Outdoor Guide, 2nd Edition

Raising Kids & Tomatoes, by Rob Kasper

Motherhood Is A Contact Sport, by Susan Reimer

Other books by Susan White-Bowden:

Everything To Live For, White-Bowden Associates, 1993

From A Healing Heart, White-Bowden Associates, 1993

Moonbeams Come At Dark Times, White-Bowden Associates, 1993

The Barn Cat, Sassy, And A Guardian Angel: Heroic Animal Tales (A Book Of Fiction For Young Readers), White-Bowden Associates, 1998

This *Baltimore Sun* book was published by SunSource, the information service of *The Sun*. To order any of the above titles or for information on research, reprints and information from the paper's archives, please call 410.332.6800.

Off**Season**

Living the retirement dream

Susan White-Bowden

with color commentary by **Jack Bowden**

THE BALTIMORE SUN

Published by
The Baltimore Sun
A Times Mirror company
501 N. Calvert Street
Baltimore, MD 21278

Edited by Melinda Greenberg
Layout and design by Jennifer Halbert
Copy edited by Ray Frager

Cover photo by Michael Orhelein, The Portrait Artist
Interior photos by Susan White-Bowden

ISBN — 1-893116-14-X
Library of Congress Control Number: 00-131718

Off Season, Living A Retirement Dream — 2000 —
Baltimore, MD: Baltimore Sun Co.: 2000

For all who pursue
their retirement dreams

Contents:

Prologue

Susan: As with most couples, Jack and I have shared some very good times and some so hard we didn't think we'd make it through.

We've had wonderful careers in television, which allowed us to meet and interview some interesting, famous and even infamous people. The high-profile, deadline driven, day-to-day existence of television news is seldom dull, often exciting, and occasionally glamorous. But for us and other reporters we worked with, it is not the pampered, elite lifestyle many viewers perceive it to be. There are, of course, exceptions.

In our personal lives, we've shared the tragedy of my son Jody's suicide, which followed the suicide of his father, $2^1/_2$ years earlier. The strength we found within ourselves and each other allowed us to go on to experience the blending of our families. My daughters became Jack's and his son became mine. And we have been blessed with six grandchildren so far. Christopher, or C.J. as he is known to everyone except us, is not yet married. We have some very dear friends, who have been with us through all these events and we've made new friends along the way.

Together we've discovered new places, new interests and new things to love about each other. We've shared the final years of my parents' lives and those of Jack's mother, who was in an assisted living facility for three years. His father died 20 years earlier. It was while my mother-in-law, Marion Bowden, was at Keswick in Baltimore that I grew close to her and learned to love her deeply. It was also during that time that I developed a writing workshop and courses for the elderly and retired students, which I now teach at area colleges and universities — most recently Johns Hopkins and Towson.

But now Jack and I are sharing a new phase of our lives, joining the 27½ million other Americans in so-called retirement. We have met many people for whom retirement from one career has meant an encore in another or the chance to explore those paths previously not taken or to revive dormant dreams. As children, most of us wanted to be something — a cowboy, a singer, an artist, a writer. Many, who didn't experience those dreams during their "prime-time" years, are making them happen now. Those are the stories of this book. It is also the story of a place that has fulfilled some of our dreams and the dreams of many others — the Delmarva coast. And that's where Jack begins the story.

Susan White-Bowden

Jack: It was the off-season at the beach and in our lives. The intensity of the prime season's heat was waning and hints of winter's big chill were in the air — the beginning of the end. But it was also simply a change of seasons, and for us a new beginning — perhaps a replenishment — like the beach swept clean by the wind and waves of all the debris accumulated during the seasons past.

There was no beach the last time I was here — the winter of 1998. A series of nor'easters had torn away most of the beach, much of the dune line and parts of some homes. I was here then as a reporter for Channel 7 in Washington, D.C., and those storms were worse than any hurricane I had covered. In television news, the more miserable and threatened you look in such storms, the better management likes it. I looked especially miserable, so they kept sending me back for

Prologue

each storm, hoping for stronger winds and bigger waves. One TV consultant even suggested that reporters should "allow themselves" to be knocked down by such winds to make it look more dramatic. It was that kind of advice that led to my decision to leave television news. Television news, unlike the people you'll meet in this book, has aged badly.

Susan left television news 10 years earlier, and has seldom been seen on the tube since. But through her books she is now seen, much more intimately, in people's minds. And with my new-found freedom, she has invited me to go that route with her. Risky! Her readers have eagerly welcomed her into their thoughts and emotions. But with me along? What's the sound of thousands of minds closing?

Jack Bowden

Chapter 1

Late
September

Susan: I want to sleep more. My eyes, still too heavy to open easily, need a conscious effort to see what the unconscious senses is on the horizon.

It is framed in the cathedral window of our third-floor garret bedroom. The vivid pinks and blues of the pre-dawn spread across the sky and reflect off of the ocean and the waves that roll onto the white sand shore.

Beside me, still sleeping soundly, is my husband of 19 years, my friend of many more. It is our first full day of our new adventure.

In June, Jack retired from television. I had left "the business" 10 years earlier. We had worked together at a Baltimore station, WMAR-TV, Channel 2, for more than 20 years.

After leaving Channel 2, Jack spent several years freelancing (narrating and hosting informational and training videos and doing some acting). But just as he began missing "the news," he was offered a full-time job with the ABC affiliate in Washington, D.C. — WJLA-TV, Channel 7. He was back in "the business" big time.

For almost eight years, he commuted more than an hour each way — starting out early in the morning and returning late at night. In addition to daily reporting, he anchored just about every newscast they had — evening, early morning and weekends. And he won an Emmy.

The time we had together then was brief, most of it spent sleeping, often in front of the television at the end of a long day. Vacations were

Late September

longed for and savored and over too quickly. But now, it is time for us and, by a providence of fate and the serendipitous intervention of a friend, we are at the beach, off-season, to realize a long-talked-about-dream.

> *Jack: My son, Christopher, who hated school, enviously describes our new venture as "an extended summer vacation, but with no required reading." He's right. It seems like a second chance at carefree youth, but with the greater wisdom acquired from all the mistakes made the first time around.*

Susan: The beach house in which we're staying for six months sits right on the sand, along the Delaware shoreline between Rehoboth Beach and Dewey Beach. Between the house and the beach, there's a protective barrier of sand dunes that forms a snug, bowl-like shield around the front porch. An abundance of tall dune grass, goldenrod, bayberries, ivy and juniper flourish in this mounded garden of sand, providing even more seclusion and privacy and making the houses on either side almost disappear.

A narrow boardwalk leads from the porch, out over the dunes, with steep steps descending to the wide public beach below and the ever-changing ocean beyond.

The three-story, weathered, brown-shingled house is called the Sea Shack by its owners. The decor, inside and out, has been done with such good taste and care that one realizes the name has been given with an endearing sense of humor. Either that or its owners live in a castle when they're not at the beach.

Montauk daisies greet us as we enter the parking area off the road. A holly tree grows from a square of earth in the pavement and a wisteria vine climbs on a trellis over the front door. The draping branches form a dramatic awning of leaves. Gazing at it, I can imagine the beauty when the vine is in bloom.

Inside, the white walls appear freshly painted and bright against the natural wood trim of the windows and doors. The ceiling is also pine, with wide unfinished wood beams that run across it in both directions. Large, floor-to-ceiling supporting beams of the same rough-milled wood stand in the middle of the first floor, allowing the living room, dining room and kitchen to share the openness of one big room. It is a room of mostly glass, with windows on three sides and a pair of large, 30-pane, French doors leading to the screened porch on the ocean side of the house. The floor of the downstairs is red terra cotta tile; upstairs the floors are all hardwood, wide plank pine, sanded to a dull natural finish.

The signature furniture, throughout the house, is antique white wicker, balanced by overstuffed chairs and sofas in fabrics of blue and white and sunny yellow. An abundance of throw pillows, placed for comfort, not for show, invite lounging, dreaming, reading or sleep.

The house's personality comes from the charm of all the interesting and colorful accents — from a collection of children's antique sand buckets and shovels grouped on top of the kitchen cabinets to antique clocks to images of mermaids on rugs and stands and on the "welcome" sign inside the entrance. There is even a metal carving of a mermaid in one of the bathrooms.

Discovering the rooms upstairs is like a treasure hunt through a three-dimensional issue of *House Beautiful*. The large front bedroom on the second floor makes the most of the ocean view. Ten windows wrap the room on three sides. Under the ones in the northeast corner, nestled next to the closet, is a cushioned window seat, big enough to stretch out on while leaning back against several more perfectly placed oversized pillows. There is enough comfort and perspective to satisfy the most passionate beach spectator. Underneath, two child-size openings have been cut in the paneling, creating a crawl space — a hideaway, equipped with mattress and toys.

Jack: We've never met the people who own this house, but, as we discover the tasteful and child-friendly decor, we form images of a warm, unpretentious and loving family. Photographs of them throughout the house and testimonials from neighbors confirm our first impressions. "I'd love to know them," Susan and I say over and over, and very quickly we feel we do.

Susan: Putting a family picture back on the dresser, we turn to the dominant feature in this room, something that takes your breath away when you walk in. It is a highly polished pine, four-poster pineapple bed that has been raised and angled to make the most of the view. With the embroidered white cotton spread and dust-ruffle skirt, the large flowered accent pillow stands out like a garden in off-season snow. There is a wicker chaise lounge, with a flower-print cushion, a natural wicker chair with a sunflower throw blanket, a sea mist blue love seat, a pine bureau, a big bookcase with current novels and books about the seashore.

We quickly dub this the guest room, perhaps not wanting to disturb the perfect display with daily use. Or maybe feeling that such elegance should be experienced only once in a while, on special occasions. Besides, it will be more fun to see the expressions on the faces of our grown children and visiting friends when we show them to "their" room. Also, climbing the stairs to the third-floor bedroom, we both decide this is the one for us. We later learned that the home's owners had made the same decision.

The third-floor garret bedroom suite is generous, with a large private bath that has a skylight and huge shower. And just off the hall, between the bedroom and bath, a door opens to a porch set in the roof. The waist-high wall ensures privacy and protection from the wind and encourages thoughts of sunbathing even during the fall and winter months. A visiting friend would later suggest that it was a perfect place for sunbathing in the buff. "Not for me," I quickly exclaimed. "At this age and stage of my life, I have too much buff for even the forgiving eyes of heaven to see."

Chapter 2

Old Friends, New Acquaintances

It is the daughter of two dear friends of mine who intervened to make the beach house ours, at least for this seasonal interval.

This "girl," Weeder Roberts Obrecht, whom I watched grow up, still calls me Aunt Susie, even though we're not related and, unfortunately, rarely see each another anymore. I was friends with her parents before she was born. Her given name was to be, and is, Elizabeth. But to the surprise of her father, who had sandy-colored hair, and her mother, a brunette, little Elizabeth came out with bright red hair. "Where did that hair come from?" everyone would say. She was jokingly labeled "a weed." She has been "Weeder" ever since, and now her oldest daughter, also named Elizabeth, is called "Posey" — a flower, her mother notes, not a weed.

Weeder continues to be a cherished friend of my oldest daughter, Marjorie. In fact, they are godmothers for each other's children. Knowing that Weeder and her husband, Andy, own a beach house in Delaware, I called her to explain what we were looking for.

"Something on the beach would be nice — but not necessary — near the beach would be fine — within walking distance to the ocean — something we could afford — with neither one of us having a salaried job — money is a consideration — perhaps we could pay per month what a house would bring per week in-season. But here's the real catch," I went on hesitantly, for fear of squelching my chances

Old Friends, New Acquaintances

before I even got started. "We have this dog." Adding very quickly before she could respond, "She's a 3-year-old yellow lab that doesn't chew anymore. She's very well-behaved, house trained and I don't allow her on furniture."

When the call came, weeks later, from California, it took me several minutes to realize it was our dream coming true. I'd almost given up that this would happen, at least not this year. "Hello, my name is Judi. My husband, Phil, and I have a beach house near the Obrechts in Dewey Beach — we only use it in the summer — we would be delighted to have someone responsible in the house through the winter — actually it will be a relief — and we don't mind that you have a dog. Better a dog than little children," this devoted mother of three young girls said with a laugh. She and I agreed on the rental, sight unseen — they hadn't seen us, and we hadn't seen their house. They trusted us, and we were so grateful to them.

And so here we are, in late September, checking it out. It is my dream come true — the house I had envisioned, the one I would have created, if I could have tailored it to my every desire. And now it will be ours from October through March, and we will be sharing it with our dog, Angel. In October we will be coming back with sweat clothes and sweaters, word processors to write with and our dog with her beach toys.

I am overwhelmed by the magnitude of our good fortune.

> *Susan's smile, which begins as soon as we see the house, grows wider as we explore the interior. I haven't seen her this happy since our annual escape from reality in Bermuda, which we both say is too expensive — until we get there, and the island works its magic, making us feel, and even look years younger — at least to each other.*

I feel like a teen-ager on a first date with the basketball star I'd secretly loved from afar. I am giddy with excitement, as we race from one room to the next, discovering its special offerings.

> *Whenever I read something such as this that Susan's written, I view it as a harmless simile — and believe that*

9

there never really was some basketball star she yearned for. You can decide if I'm very secure or very naive.

As I check the views from each window, I see two people coming up the beach from the Obrechts' house. It's Weeder's father and his wife, a woman I've never met. Weeder had told me they'd be visiting from Ohio and staying at her beach house. The excitement of this day is growing, and cannot be contained. "Come on!" I call out to Jack, "Pere's out front." (Pere is pronounced Perry — his name, actually it's his middle name, is Peregrine.) Jack has only met Pere once, years ago. It was a casual meeting, at a party. They exchanged hardly more than a handshake and a smile, but also a knowing nod, each man acknowledging that the other is special to me, and glad for it.

It has been so many years since Pere and I have talked, really talked. So much has changed. There have been divorces and deaths, remarriages, additional children and now grandchildren. Our first marriages were casualties of marrying too young and the dramatic social changes of the 1960s and 1970s. Women wanted more, and when we got it, what we'd had didn't fit into the new picture of who we'd become. While some men got twisted and often broken trying to adhere to the old male role of dominance as they struggled to embrace newly evolving women as their equals, other men, such as Jack and Pere, seem to have emerged stronger, more sensitive, with an enhanced respect for women and themselves. Although many old relationships crumbled, those that survived, and the new ones established on firmer, more equitable ground, will perhaps endure with less gender competition or role playing.

Geography also came between us; no longer do we live in the same state. Pere was away when my first husband, his friend, John, committed suicide. And he was gone when my son, Pere's godson, followed John's example 2$^1/_2$ years later. Pere is now remarried, and I haven't had a chance to witness his new happiness, nor he mine with Jack.

Our past seems like another lifetime, but now our paths are crossing again, perhaps on a more appreciative plane. I've learned that friendships that can endure without constant nourishment and can be renewed without strain or pretense are the most special kind.

The hair under the baseball cap is now gray instead of sandy brown. The suntanned flesh over his broad chest seems less firm than I remember. The

Old Friends, New Acquaintances

furrows around his mouth are new. My hand moves across my own lined lips and fleshy chin, as I call out to him.

"Is that Pere Roberts out there?" He bolts over the dunes, with the athletic exuberance I remember, and I run to meet him. Pere folds me into his powerful arms. My heart seems to stop in a suspension of time, as we cling together for one breathless moment. Separating, I can see in his eyes that Pere shares my thoughts of the past, but we both move quickly on, for fear of dampening this euphoric moment with feelings of sadness and regret that could so easily be brought to the surface.

There is no need to speak of it, at least not now.

"Susie White, my God, you look great!" Pere always was good for my ego. "Oh my, it's good to see you," he gushes. The introductions are tossed out, relaxed and informal.

"Jack — you remember Pere."

"Of course."

"And this is my wife, Phyllis. Weeder and the gang call her Honey."

"Honey?" Jack and I ask in unison.

"Yes," Pere replies, obviously relishing the chance to retell a story he loves. "One day Phyllis was talking to our granddaughter, Posey, about our large extended family and where everyone fit in. She asked Posey if she thought she, Phyllis, was her grandmother. 'No,' said Posey emphatically, 'you're not my grandmother; you're Grandfather's Honey.'"

We all laugh, including Phyllis, who says, "That's always been good enough for me."

Laughter is such a good barometer of friendships or relationships. The easier it comes, the more comfortable the tie. The four of us laugh often over the next 24 hours, usually prodded by Pere's unassuming wit. He tells us about his new grandchild, who is his first grandson.

"They named him Chancellor Carroll Roberts," he says matter-of-factly.

"Chancellor?" Jack responds, sounding impressed.

Pausing, with the deft timing of a perfectly delivered punchline, Pere says, "Yeah, it didn't come off any tombstone in our family."

Pere and Phyllis take us under their wings, showing us around Rehoboth, a town they're more familiar with than we are, because they have visited Weeder so often. Jack and I have always vacationed in north Ocean City or Fenwick Island, only occasionally making our way farther up the coast to Bethany. Now, discovering the best restaurants, shops and local gathering places of Rehoboth and Dewey Beach will be part of our new adventure.

First, they take us up to the quaint little town of Lewes. (Pronounced, the locals tell us, Lewis, but many say Looz.)

However you pronounce it, Pere and Phyllis want to be the ones to introduce us to its charm. "The first town in the first state," the welcome signs boast. We rush to arrive shortly after 5 p.m. for the early-bird special — a complete lobster dinner for $11.95. It's well worth hurrying for, with sumptuous bread, salad and something we've never had before, but will again — french fried sweet potatoes, with a honey, butter, brown sugar sauce.

Most area restaurants, in the off-season, have either early-bird specials or special nights during the week when they reduce prices on many or all of their entrees. Retired people all over the country are quick to discover this money-saving practice, and now we've joined their ranks. Our younger friends kid us about doing "The Senior Citizen Things," but when they visit, they clearly enjoy the bargains. It's not only the savings we're enjoying: it's also dining out at an early hour. Until a few months ago, we'd be lucky to get dinner at home by 8:30 and were rarely able to go out for dinner, because of a lack of time, not money. Now, we have the time and the money — less money, but with these discounted dinners it will go farther.

Another discovery we make, with a great sense of relief, at this first off-season dinner is that there will be no haggling over who will pay the bill. Without comment, Jack and Pere hand the waitress two credit cards and ask her to charge half the check to each one.

Retirement brings a new set of rules about finances and what's socially acceptable behavior, making situations concerning money more comfortable for everyone. All of a sudden, the playing field has been leveled, whether you once owned your own company or simply worked for one. Most of us are now, as they say, "on fixed incomes." Perhaps we'll find that although we have less money, we'll have more fun with what we have.

Chapter 3

Finding a **niche**
The Writers

Just off the back porch, situated snugly between the ridge of the protective dunes and the shrubbery in front of the porch are two pockets of soft, powdery sand. They fan out from each side of the narrow boardwalk that leads out over the dunes to the beach. In one of these private beach areas I set up two beach chairs and two cushioned lounge chairs that I'd recently bought at a yard sale in Dewey Beach.

I'd never been to a yard sale. Previously, I'd either been too busy going somewhere when I passed them by, or thought, "If they don't want what's being sold, why should I? I already have enough junk of my own at home." But this was different. I wasn't rushing anywhere — just out to get the morning papers and there was lots of time, say about six months, to do whatever I wanted. And there, sitting on someone's lawn, with a lot of other stuff, were two perfectly good — lovely, in fact — lounge chairs. The cushions, striped, aqua, coral and beige, were worn, but there were no stains or rips. "Just what we need," I said excitedly to my dog, Angel, sitting beside me in the car.

"And would you believe they were only $7 apiece?" I told my daughter Marjorie that night on the phone. She laughed at my excitement. "And I got a water dish for Angel for 50 cents — and I got four crystal wine glasses, that have never been used, for $1 apiece.

"What have I been telling you all these years?" my daughter scolded. "You don't have to buy new to get exactly what you need or have been looking for," she laughed as she lectured.

Retirement begins...

"But," I protested, "you didn't tell me saving money could be so much fun."

The chairs in the sandy niche, protected from the off-season winds, create the perfect sanctuary for talking, reading, writing or just doing nothing. Somehow, at the beach, just sitting and watching the tides roll in and out seems OK. At home, on the farm, with so many chores, sitting seems lazy and irresponsible.

We've come to the beach for two reasons: to have a change of lifestyle and to do some writing together, as well as separately. Whether it's The Great American Novel, thoughts and reflections or just postcards to the kids, it doesn't matter, as long as we do it together and enjoy it, it will be worthwhile. Without the daily deadlines of television news, we'll be happy. We've both had enough of that to last the rest of our lives. If we don't write at all that, too, will be okay. We're here for us. This is "our time."

I admit I indulge in more "doing nothing days" than Susan does. As the unseasonably warm weather extends deep into the fall, she looks at me lazing in the sun and expresses some variation of "I guess you'll start writing tomorrow?" It isn't exactly writer's block —

more like sun block. The weather makes life at the beach so perfect that work seems an unappreciative waste of a rare gift.

Jack points out an ad in the newspaper in which Henry David Thoreau is quoted. "Go confidently in the direction of your dreams. Live the life you imagined." Living in this beach house, off-season, is the life we imagined. As for the rest of the dream — writing — Jack says he's confident that Thoreau wouldn't allow such a "goal" to get in the way of the experience. "Mark it down as research," Jack says, "quiet research."

It seems to me that approaching retirement is very similar to establishing a career as a young adult. I believe each individual, as well as each couple, must find what works and what is personally satisfying. I think we all need to ask and answer the question: "What, based on what is affordable, will make me happy and will cause me the fewest regrets later?"

My father, a dentist, worked until he was 82. His dental patients were as close as family and he enjoyed visiting with them as much as continuing to care for them. It was also very rewarding for him to know he was still needed and productive. And he enjoyed being told by those who did his lab work, such as making the crowns he had prepared, that even at his age, "no one did it better," and, his patients added, "cheaper." He was there for them, and he was saving them money. One patient told me, "Your dad is my inflation fighter." They loved him. He even made house calls on patients who were incapacitated.

My mother served as my father's secretary/receptionist for 40 years. She was with him in the office every day, all day. It was my mother's dream that my father would retire so that they could travel more. And from age 75 on, he kept promising he was going to do it, "next year." When my mother died suddenly of heart failure at age 82, my father sobbed with regret. He kept saying over and over again, "Why didn't I retire? We were going to take a cruise around the world. Why didn't I do it? I thought we had time."

My father worked too long, but it also wouldn't have made him happy to have retired at age 65. Some people need the routine and reward of a daily job, even when they can afford not to do it. As I'm writing this, 77-year-old Senator/astronaut John Glenn is orbiting the Earth. His daughter said in a TV interview that she has never seen her father happier than he was as he trained and prepared for this historic flight.

Recently, I ran into a former executive with McCormick, the large, international spice company headquartered in Baltimore. I once did some public relations work for that company. This executive told me he had retired from McCormick, but was now working for another, much smaller, local spice company that had a very limited market area, but was growing. He seemed excited and energized as he told me how this came about.

"The day after I retired, I got up, had breakfast, read the paper and then said to myself, 'Now what do I do?'" He told me that he went to talk to the owners of the small spice company. They were interested in expanding, but weren't sure how to go about it.

"We'd love to have someone with your experience guiding us," they said, "but we could never afford to pay you what you're used to or deserve." He said to them, "You write a figure down on a piece of paper what you could afford to pay me. On another piece of paper I'll write down what I'd be willing to work for, and we'll see if we can get together."

As the executive went on to finish the story, his eyes sparkled and he grinned broadly. "I'd written $1 on my piece of paper, so I went to work for what they had written on theirs." He went on proudly, "It is now the fastest-growing spice company in the country, and we're about to build a new manufacturing plant."

"What about your wife?" I asked. "How does she feel about your second career?"

His smile broadened, "She plays golf every day, and I mean every day — she couldn't be happier."

At a beautiful bed and breakfast in Bucks County, Pa., that Jack and I visited, we met a man who has used retirement to combine work and play, but in a totally different setting than he had before.

It was just after sunrise. Pulling aside the lace curtains in our room, I watched with interest as this man carefully pruned the roses in the formal garden of the inn. A handsome man, with gray hair and mustache, he looked youthful in the soft early morning light. Dressed in a blue golf shirt and pressed khaki pants, he was, I assumed, the owner of the inn, whom we hadn't met.

After breakfast, strolling the gardens, I stopped to chat with the man, and to admire his gardens. He pointed out with pride the numerous lush varieties of flowering plants. It turned out that he was not the owner, but the gardener and landscape designer. He worked in this garden almost every morning and played golf several afternoons a week, the two things he loved doing most.

Before retirement, he owned and ran two businesses in Philadelphia, and he and his wife owned a big home in the exclusive "Mainline" section of the city. They had long loved the Bucks County area and vowed to live there in retirement. They sold the Philadelphia businesses and house and bought a smaller Bucks County home that needed restoring.

The restoration, primarily under the wife's guidance, had been fun, a new challenge, and was continuing.

He told me that he and his wife developed a friendship with the couple who owned the inn, and he had offered to help with the major landscaping planned for the sadly neglected gardens. The innkeepers gratefully accepted, but, because what was needed was so extensive, insisted it be a business arrangement.

This man agreed on a flat fee — a yearly retainer, enabling him to set his own hours. He worked when the garden needed his attention and played golf when it didn't.

Providing another variation on this theme are Ruth Ann and Bill Krauss of Newark, Del., and Dewey Beach, whose daughter, Judi, along with her husband, owns the beach house we're renting. We met Ruth Ann and Bill shortly after we arrived. They also own a cottage in this area, and were closing it up for the winter when they dropped by to introduce themselves. They are a youthful couple displaying a wealth of energy, interest and good humor. She's 68, he's 71.

Dr. William Krauss has a degree in veterinary medicine. For 15 years, he taught at the University of Delaware, and then spent the next 15 years conducting veterinary research for the DuPont Company. However, it was when he retired from DuPont that Bill finally began to live the life of which he had always dreamed.

Bill's first love was music. He had played the clarinet in high school and college, but felt that to try to earn a living as a musician would be a struggle that wouldn't be fair to the woman he loved even more than music, Ruth Ann, whom he met in college and married the day she graduated. Even though his music was, in Ruth Ann's words, "Pushed to the

Retirement begins...

very back burner," they created a wonderful life together, especially when Bill was chairman of the department at the University of Delaware. Ruth Ann said fondly, "The house was always filled with students, teacher's assistants, lab helpers and grad students — we had a blast. The music definitely didn't start bubbling until retirement,"

But retirement gave Bill Krauss the opportunity he'd been waiting for, and he did more than just stir the pot. In 1989, as soon as he left Dupont, he auditioned for and was hired by the Newark Symphony Orchestra, and at age 62 he began living the life he had imagined. "When you play with a good orchestra," Bill told me, "and ours is a good one, the rewards are tremendous."

In a recent concert, Bill was called on to accompany an opera singer who was making a guest appearance. After the performance, she said to Bill, "You're the first clarinetist in my entire career who has played that piece to suit me, in the absolute right tempo."

"That," Bill said to me, "was one of the biggest thrills of my life."

And Ruth Ann is also now honing skills that previously lay dormant while she worked in her profession, as a teacher, and while they raised their two children — a son named Rick and daughter Judi.

She has volunteered as a hospice worker and in the emergency room of the Newark hospital. But it is in the basement of their Newark home, in her workshop, using tiny tools and an artistic eye, that she builds doll houses — beautifully crafted, precisely cut, glued and painted Victorian and Colonial doll houses. At this point, she doesn't sell them; she builds them simply for the pleasure of doing it. Of course, several have gone to their grandchildren.

As with most retired couples, grandchildren claim a great deal of the Krausses' time and thought. In counseling one grandchild, Ruth Ann described life as being like the intertwining of a braid. "There are three parts that make up the whole," she told the child. "One strand represents what you are born with. The second is what happens to you, circumstances over which you have no control. The third is what you make of your life, how you handle what you are born with and what happens to you, the good and the bad. It is the third strand that can secure the braid or allow the whole to fall apart. We have choices," she said with the wisdom of experience. Ruth Ann and Bill Krauss have turned their over-60 years into a rewarding braid of life. Using talents they were born with, the good health and opportunities they're lucky to be experiencing at this age, they have chosen to pursue and live to the fullest their retirement dreams.

> *Unfortunately, some people view retirement as "so little time; so little to do." For us, and most of the retirees we know, it's just the opposite. Two of our friends from television — Channel 7 reporter Ed Turney, of "Turney's Journeys" fame, and Jack Miller, a Channel 2 news cameraman (in the business we call them shooters) — want to cut back, but don't want to leave the news business completely, as Susan and I have.*
>
> *Ed, who is a couple of years younger than I am, left Channel 7 a few months after I did, but now works part-time there, continuing his popular and fully sponsored "Reach the Beach" series during the spring and summer. But that still leaves him and his wife plenty of time to fish and enjoy their new boat and retirement home in Ocean City, with their grown children and grandchildren.*
>
> *Jack Miller, who has been at Channel 2 for almost 37 years, wants to work less, perhaps taking his pension and Social Security early and maybe working two or three days a week, leaving four or five days for golf, tennis and more time with his wife, Roxanne, and his first grandchild.*
>
> *Incidentally, Jack is the kind of friend who insists that we play golf together, even though he hits in the 80s and I hit in the 100s. However, recently, before we played, Jack spent several hours with me working on my swing, and telling me that I was really quite good, but I'm not sure if he was trying to convince me or himself. Most older golfers try to hit their ages — instead I'll settle for the temperature. That way, a score of 100-plus means I'm really hot.*

Here at the beach, it's a blue-sky October day. Jack and I are spending the morning in the lounge chairs, soaking up the sun. I'm writing in my spiral notebook, my favorite way to write, and he's reading the newspapers. Jack enjoys reading at least four newspapers a day: *The Sun, The Washington Post, The Wall Street Journal,* our local paper at home, *The Carroll County Times*, and now the Delaware papers. Jack takes a break for lunch, and when he returns with a book in his hand, he quips, "I wrote one line while I was inside. Does that count?" I can tell by his expression and his tone of voice that it's a good line. He is pleased. I smile, sharing his accomplishment, "That counts."

> *Actually the conversation was not that short or that sweet. "But," Susan continued, "is that one line for our book, or is it for one of your books, your movie script, your TV script or your essays?" We both laughed at her summary of my overly ambitious, sporadic and, thus far, unfocused writing ambitions. "Our book," I replied. Susan understood. "Our book" is not this book, but a novel, which is still in the plotting stage. Several years back, while I was still working in Washington and when we were still just dreaming of renting a beach house and writing together, as well as being together, we began talking about "our novel," partially plotting it and fleshing out some of the characters.*
>
> *And then our dream came true — except for one thing: I began working on the novel, but Susan began writing about our experience here. She simply said it seemed so right, she couldn't resist, and pleaded with me to do it with her. I kept insisting that I didn't have time with all the other things I was writing. She pointed out, unfairly I thought, that aside from stacks of scribbled notes, I hadn't actually started writing anything. And when I pointed out that I also wasn't comfortable writing about myself, she threatened to write things about me that would make me even more uncomfortable.*
>
> *And so I tried, but after several pages it didn't seem right to me. I went for a long run along the beach; came back and told Susan, "I'm sorry, I can't do this; I'm just not comfortable — I want to write fiction."*
>
> *Susan said she understood, although I could see the disappointment on her face.*

He stood before me nervously, as if he had something life-altering to tell me, some disturbing confession he had to make, like leaving me for another, much younger, woman. (Leaving me for another woman would be one thing, a much younger woman would be life-threatening — for him!) What he saw on my face was actually relief, that it was only writing I'd be doing alone.

So, that's how it went for several weeks — she wrote this book, and I worked on the novel and some other projects. However, when I began to proofread her work (she's asked me to edit all her books) I began to get caught up in it, and at a couple of places in her copy I wrote my point of view on something she had written.

Later, as she went through the changes I had made, I heard her chuckle, and she came over to me, smiling, and asked, "Do you want me to put this in the book?" "No," I said, "I was just trying to get a rise out of you." "But why not?" she said. "It's kind of 'she said — he said' like the exchanges we used to have on the air, when we anchored the news together; the viewers loved it, and so did I." "Well, of course, you did," I said, "the viewers always took your side." "Just try it," she said. And so I did, and as the book progressed, so did my contribution to it and my enthusiasm for it. She was right, as usual. And I soon realized that working with her, on anything, was wonderful. We were writing and laughing and enjoying the beach — together. We were living our dream.

As you read on, you will see that Jack's contribution evolves from comments to paragraphs to entire chapters.

In the beginning she kept telling me, "The book needs more of you in it." Toward the end, as I handed her additional pages, she would look at me, unsmiling now, and simply say, "More?"

Chapter 4

Beach Time

I set up two writing stations in the beach house; both have word processors and a view. Mine, which I claimed the very first day, is in front of the big expanse of window in the dining area of the first floor. It overlooks the porch, the sandy cove, with the grouping of chairs, and the dunes in front and on either side. Through a break in the tall dune grasses, I can see the beach and the ocean stretching to the horizon. At this moment, dolphins swim by not 50 feet offshore. For the most part this time of year, the beach and my view are void of people. Occasionally, however, someone will walk through the scene, often with a dog, and I pause to watch until he or she disappears behind the dunes. In a little while, he reappears, heading back to the part of the beach where he began — drifters through my tapestry of water, waves, blowing grasses and sand.

For Jack, I moved a table and desk chair behind the living room couch. He also faces the beach and has a panoramic view, provided by the whole front wall of windows.

The only problem with working at home, or in this case our home away from home with a wonderful view, is that as soon as you wake up, you're at work.

So far, I've spent most of the time at my station staring at the view,

Beach Time

marveling at its majesty. How could anyone ever tire of the endless changes of light? The dramatic colors of sunrise over the ocean, the vividness of midday and, later, the muted hues cast indirectly by the setting sun behind us — that soft light that many photographers wait for. Even without photographs, the visions are surely etched in my mind to savor at some future time.

When I do write, it is with a pen and my notebook while I sit in one of the lounge chairs, because it is much too sunny and warm to stay inside. I can feed my scribbled thoughts into the word processor later, when the cold envelops the shore. Although it is near the end of October, every day has been warm enough for shorts and sunscreen.

This past weekend crowds jammed the town of Rehoboth Beach for Halloween activities dubbed "The Seawitch Festival." Hundreds of people marched in the annual costume parade, while an estimated 20,000 people lined the streets to watch. The 70-degree weather also brought many of those people out onto the beach. Unexpectedly warm weather in October almost always results in squealing children trying to brave the chilly ocean for one last swim of the season. An occasional adult also finds the lure of the rolling waves too tempting to resist. One such man was a 75-year-old neighbor in our new beach community.

I was sitting on the beach with Weeder, Andy, their children and a few of their beach friends, all down for the weekend events. Jack and his son, Christopher, who was visiting us to celebrate his 28th birthday, had gone to get lunch. Christopher's girlfriend, Melissa Mackinnon, headed out for a run along the edge of the ocean.

It was then that our older neighbor and his wife returned to our circle of chairs from their long, energetic stroll up the beach. "A swim would feel good," someone suggested. "Yeah!" The kids cheered and chanted, "Can we, can we?" Andy got up out of his chair and peeled off his shirt. He had thought ahead and worn bathing trunks. "What about you?" Andy said to the older man, "you're always up for a dip in the ocean."

"I don't have a bathing suit on," the septuagenarian protested half-heartedly, the excitement in his eyes belying his own excuse. And before anyone could suggest that it would only take him a few minutes to run home and change, he was pulling off his shirt and stripping off his long pants.

Weeder hid her face, "I don't want to see this," she said, as he jogged

Beach Time

toward the ocean in his underwear. "I don't want to have anything to do with this," his wife said, as she headed back to their house.

I looked over at Weeder, who was lying face down on her towel, her hands still half-covering her eyes, peeking up at me. Her look seemed to ask, "What's happening now? Tell me what's going on."

"He's wearing white briefs," I informed her, "thin white briefs — wait till they get wet." She dropped her head, laughing into the sand.

Melissa returned, hot and sweaty, from an hour-long run. Unaware of what was going on, she pulled off her shirt and turned toward the water. "I'm going in," she called out, running back across the sand, diving quickly into a rising wave. She had on her black running shorts and midriff top. "Bathing suits are a thing of the past," I quipped. "They seem to be today," Weeder replied, with a girlish giggle. "Oh my God — he's coming out," I warned. "Oh boy, they are really thin white briefs," Weeder's face turned red, and she laughed so hard her body shook. So did I. "At least there's a thick panel in front," I said, trying to give her a complete mental image.

Melissa, who now had a rear view of him as he waded out of the water, stood chin deep, staring, waves crashing around her, a look of disbelief on her face.

Weeder buried her head deeper into her hands as he stood over her, oblivious to his near nudity, drying off with a towel before wrapping it around his waist.

"Spontaneity," the 75-year-old said, with a boyish grin, "that's what makes life fun. Do the unexpected, and it'll keep you young."

Chapter 5

Holding on, Letting Go

The weather continues to be sunny and mild, defiantly delaying the inevitable change that off-season dictates — tempting people to revise their plans and stay. The elaeagnus bushes on either side of our porch are blooming again. The seductive scent permeates the air around them. Bees, aroused from dormancy, swarm in appreciation.

The unseasonable warmth means unwanted mosquitoes can also extend their hunt for human blood. Clouds of them rise up from the dune plants and attack. I engage them with bug spray, but they force me to retreat. Eventually, an overnight drop in temperature stops them. Incidentally, entomologists say that it's only the female mosquitoes that bite. There is nothing to fear from the males of the species. They simply spend there entire lives keeping the blood-thirsty females happy.

The sky remains a clear, cloud-free blue. A gentle breeze sways the dune grasses about with the softness of a summer wind. There is no hint of the harsh winds that are certain to come soon. It is perfect. So why am I feeling down?

We're going home for a visit, leaving this lovely sanctuary. I fight the mood with self-recrimination, telling myself I'm a spoiled ingrate. I have the family farm, which my daughters and their families share, living in the two houses on either side of ours. It provides Jack and me the opportunity to be an integral part of our grandchildren's lives. We've always had the advantage of seeing them every day, not just on holidays or special occasions. And while here at the beach we've missed them, still I don't want to leave, to go back home — back to reality. Reality is rarely a day at the beach.

Our home is only a three-hour drive from the Delaware shore, so we decided, when we began this adventure, that we would go back every two weeks to collect the mail, pay bills and deal with any needs or problems that might have cropped up in our absence. Based on past vacation experiences, we knew there would always be "something" to handle when we returned. I'd jokingly said to friends, when explaining we'd be returning home at regular intervals, that "you can't just walk away from an old farmhouse with leaky pipes." On our first visit back in October, the first thing I did was check the cellar, and, sure enough, there was a fine stream of water spewing from a pinhole leak in a copper hot-water pipe. The muddy mess it had created (the old-fashioned farmhouse cellar has an earthen floor) indicated that it had probably been spraying most of the time we were away.

I rushed upstairs to make a frantic phone call for help to Jim the plumber, one of the two men in my life I refer to as "my significant other."

Neither of whom is her husband. There's some pride in being one of a kind.

The other and first significant other is Gil, a neighbor who helps with the farm machinery, the horses and digging us out when we get buried in snow. My relationship with these two men is unconditional. When I call Jim or Gil, he comes without questions or excuses. Jack gladly steps aside for them, because he doesn't know a thing about plumbing or machinery and he's the rare male willing to admit it.

No comment.

The simple solution would be to shut off all the water in the house when we go away. However, we can't do that, because we have hot-water baseboard heat, and in the winter the heat needs to be on, at least 50 degrees, or those pipes will freeze. Plus, throughout the year, the water line running from our house to the barn watering trough needs to be on for the horses. So each time, we go back with trepidation, unsure of what we might find. Which probably explains my mood on this day.

> *I don't want to leave the beach either, and I walk out across the dunes to meet Susan as she returns from walking Angel. "What a beautiful day," I say, "Sure you don't want to spend a little time on the beach before we leave?"*

I resist. We're driving both cars back so that I can leave mine home for the winter. I'm afraid my 10-year-old Jeep will turn into a bucket of rust sitting all winter in the salt air.

I want to leave at noon so we can avoid the rush hour traffic on the Baltimore Beltway. I need to have Jack follow me up the road, in case my old car breaks down. "I'd really like to get home by 3, 3:30, maybe 4 at the latest," I plead apologetically. He seems reluctant, and like a child trying to delay bedtime, says, "I'm just going to take a short walk up the beach," and heads out across the sand. When he gets back, there is lunch to fix and last-minute things to do: sweeping, laundry to fold and the garbage to take out. "We have to leave this house in order, in case something happens and we don't get back," Jack says to justify the further delay. We leave at 2 p.m.

On the way up the road, I keep checking the rear-view mirror to make sure he's behind me, and he's always there. However, after we get on the Baltimore Beltway, in heavy rush-hour traffic, I glance in the mirror, but don't see Jack's car. When I can, I change lanes. I still can't see his car. After I exit onto 795, I have a chance to pull onto the shoulder to allow him to catch up. I activate my flashers and wait. "Where is he?" I say to Angel.

My aggravation turns to concern. "He could have been in an accident and I wouldn't even know it," I think. An emergency vehicle with flashing lights passes, heading in that direction. I don't have a car phone, but Jack does, so I get off at the next exit to find a phone.

The traffic is hopelessly bogged down. My stomach churns as I allow panic to creep in. "What if something has happened — just

Holding On, Letting Go

when we're getting this chance for a new life together?"

The line of cars I'm in inches forward. The ones on the right, turning south onto Reisterstown Road, are going faster. I wanted to go north toward home. Maybe I can find a phone quicker by going with the faster flow of traffic. I cut between cars.

Horns blow: I ignore them. At the next intersection, I make an illegal U-turn into a shopping center where I locate a phone. My mouth is dry, my heart's in my throat, as I listen to the ringing of the car phone. "Hello," Jack answers calmly.

"Where are you?" I ask anxiously. "What happened to you? You disappeared. I waited for you. You never caught up."

"Oh," he says, seeming surprised at my concern, "I got off to go to the bakery. I thought you saw me. The bakery was closed. I'm almost home. Where are you?"

Jack follows his sweet tooth as slavishly as our lab Angel follows her nose.

You're probably thinking that Susan would have been better off if something had happened to me. But she wasn't even angry, just relieved that I was all right. Amazing, isn't it? I was worried that writing about myself would be difficult — reading about myself is even worse.

(Try living with him.) Driving onto the road to the farm, the first thing I see is that our entrance sign is lying on the ground; it appears someone has backed into it and knocked it down. Trash blows about; apparently, the neighbor's dog has been into the garbage cans again. I'm irritated that no one has picked it up, something I always do when I'm home. These aren't good omens; I feel myself tightening.

At home, Angel and I jump out of the car. The dog, happy to be home, without any of my conflicting thoughts about when we might escape back to the beach, runs excitedly to reacquaint herself with the familiar sights and scents of the farm. She races, with tail wagging, to greet my daughters' dogs, one of which is her brother. She tears out to the barn, jumping into the watering trough to cool off after her three-hour car ride on this warm day.

Homecoming for Angel is carefree.

In contrast, I race for the cellar to check the pipes. There are no leaks this time, and I start to feel relieved, until I walk into the house. Jack is coming down the steps, and there is a puzzled look of concern on his face. "Somebody's been upstairs. I don't know if someone's broken in or what. The window's open on the third floor — and it appears that someone has just taken a shower in the second-floor bathroom — it's a mess."

"Why would anyone break in to take a shower?" I think, as I rush to look.

The bathroom is saturated. Water clings to the walls and the ceiling. Puddles have formed on the floor. Beads of water hang on the mirror and on the ceiling inside the linen closet. The paint on the inside of the door, which had been closed, is bubbled from moisture. The folded towels on the racks are soaked. Rivulets run down the walls. The sink and shelves are coated with mildew.

It turns out that one of our grandsons had been using that bathroom for long, very hot showers when there was a water problem at his house, but left the bathroom closed up, not allowing it to dry out. He and our other grandsons had opened the third-floor window while playing up there, and forgot to close it.

As I stand looking at the mess, I begin to feel overwhelmed. "I don't know," I say to myself. "I don't know if it's worth it. You go away, but when you come back, there are so many problems and things to deal with." I fight the tears welling up in my eyes. When our grandsons come in after they get home from school, I express to them the frustrations I'm feeling.

"So don't go away." Tommy says matter-of-factly. His comment makes me smile, because he doesn't like my being away. He didn't want me to go in the first place.

Jack goes to the store to get food for dinner, and I begin to tackle the mess in the bathroom and go through the mound of mail.

The phone rings. I answer it with hesitation. It's my stepson, Christopher. "Hey! Susie Sunshine, what's happening?" He is calling to talk to his father and to confirm plans for the dinner party we are having for my daughter O'Donnell's 40th birthday at Rudy's 2900 restaurant. Something to look forward to on this trip home. In the course of the conversation, I go through the whole litany of my day.

"I don't know," I say, sounding defeated, "maybe Tommy's right. Maybe we shouldn't go away. Maybe we should just stay here, take

Holding On, Letting Go

care of problems on a daily basis — perhaps prevent some of them from happening. Sometimes, I think this is the way it's supposed to be — that you're not supposed to enjoy life. It's not supposed to be stress free."

"Whoa," he pops back at me, "it's that kind of negative thinking that keeps people from doing anything — from getting anywhere. That's what makes people settle for what they think is their 'lot in life.' It's precisely that kind of thinking that kills all creativity and imagination. That's not like you."

He's right; it's not like me. But having so much, sometimes I feel guilty, greedy to want more. It's not that I'm not appreciative — I am, and I always try to give back. I guess I'm just questioning if it's selfish to want to have this time with Jack at the beach.

"Hey," Christopher continues, "things happen, problems occur, wherever you are. Sure, they might accumulate while you're away — so what? You take care of them, and you go on. Come on, Susie, I've seen you deal with a lot worse than this."

He's right. I hang up and start opening the mail with new energy and a more positive attitude, as I continue to build on my stepson's reasoning.

Certainly, we should be able to divide our lives between both worlds for a while. And the grandchildren help make that possible — feeding the horses and barn cats, bringing in the mail and generally looking out for things. One soaked bathroom is not a bad tradeoff for all that.

Jack returns with the groceries and a bouquet of flowers. It's a bunch of fall chrysanthemums, daisies and three little sunflowers that resemble black-eyed Susans, the flower my son used to pick for me.

"After the rough day you've had, I thought these might cheer you up," Jack says, kissing me on the forehead.

Now I feel guilty for being upset over such insignificant, unimportant things. I am so lucky. "I love you," I whisper.

The next day, the plumber comes and decides that the most effective and economical way to solve our leaky pipe problem and to avoid unauthorized showers, is to run one new water pipe to the heating system, with a connection to feed the barn.

"Then," he says, "you can shut off all the rest of the water in the house."

"Yes," I cheer, jumping up and down, "Do it — just do it."

And isn't that what my stepson was saying? Solve the problems that block progress and growth and go back to the beach.

Chapter 6

Change

There is no glorious sunrise on this day at the beach — no pinks and blues, no blinding ball of red gold coming up out of the ocean. There are only shades of gray outside the window by my bed. But graceful gulls drift by in the fog, seeming to float on the thick, salty air. In spite of the gray, I feel no chill penetrating the panes of glass as I slip out of my gown and into my clothes.

Outside with Angel for our morning commune with nature, I marvel at the continued warmness. It is Nov. 20, and the temperature is in the 60s. The array of fall colors seem out of sync with the weather.

At home, a thick carpet of gold lies under the four big maples on the north side of our house. There has been no strong northwest wind to sweep the leaves away. I'm hoping that will happen before our next visit home.

The variety of trees and color here is surprising, and most of the transformed foliage still hangs on the branches. Usually in a beach town, autumn brings only subtle change to the basic shades of greens and browns, and that has begun here. The dune grasses have faded. The goldenrod is dying out and going to seed, its flowers now fuzzy and the color of sand.

Eventually, as with milkweed and dandelions, the goldenrod's seeds will separate and drift on the wind, but, for now, they cling tenaciously to the brown stems. The dune vegetation has been transformed into

Change

dried arrangements, which are easily swayed by the breezes and bent by the winds, yet held firm by deep roots, protecting the dunes from severe winter storms and reserving their location for spring. The pines, just off the dunes, shed old needles and cones onto the sand. These are usually the only colors of change at the seashore.

However, autumn in Rehoboth offers more than other beach towns, because here there are many varieties of deciduous trees, as well as the usual pines and hollies. The reasons, I learn, are these:

This is one of the few seashore resorts along the Atlantic coast that does not have a body of water separating the town and beach from the mainland. There is no inlet, bay or wetlands to cross before entering Rehoboth, no bridge connecting the mainland to beachfront property. South into Dewey, where Rehoboth Bay begins, the topography changes and those changes continue down the coast through Virginia, the Carolinas, Georgia, as well as up the coast, north of Rehoboth, into New England. Most oceanfront towns are on islands or peninsulas.

As a result of Rehoboth's unique location and topography, the normal reseeding and growth of indigenous trees and shrubs have spread almost to the ocean. This is the first place I've ever walked the beach and found large autumnal leaves — maple, oak, dogwood — being washed ashore with the shells.

Another reason for the large variety of trees is that many people live here year-round and have landscaped their lawns and properties extensively. And because the soil is suitable for plant growth, almost right up to the beach, they flourish.

Certainly there are not the panoramic woodland views — bordering fields and pastures — that we have at home. There is not the reflective beauty of the tree-lined reservoir that rims our farm.

But here, each splash of color, the cut-leaf red maple, the rosy hues of the Japanese cherry or the rust of the oak, stands out against the native canvas of holly and pine. It becomes the focal point of the landscape and perhaps is appreciated all the more. In the front yard of one lovely large Rehoboth house on Silver Lake, the bright mustard-colored and distinct fan-shaped leaves of a mature ginkgo tree commands the admiration of all who pass by.

This year, Jack and I comment that without the coloration of the leaves, the entire month of November might very well slip by unnoticed. Out on the beach, it just about has.

Nov. 11, almost Thanksgiving, but the day begins warm — 70 degrees — and stays that way; the temperature eventually climbs near 80. The sky is a soft blue and cloudless, except on the horizon, which is a grayish blue, and topped by cumulus clouds, resembling a snowcapped mountain range. The waves' foamy crests glisten in the sun.

We are the only ones on the beach, and most of the houses are shuttered. It's as if summer has returned, but no one has noticed except Susan and me.

I had planned to work out at the gym, but the weather is perfect for running, which takes only about a half-hour, instead of an hour-and-a-half inside a weight room, leaving more time for just sitting on the beach. Such weather is a gift that must not be wasted.

On this lovely fall afternoon — long before cocktail time — I open a nice Cabernet and savor a glass of it in the warm, summer-like sun — truly a bonus in off-season that also comes without the summer-like crowds.

Change

Sunday, Nov. 15 — sunny and warm, too warm for the sweaters, sweat shirts and jackets people wear to the beach on this day. So they tie them around their waists as they walk the water's edge. Some people carry their shoes and splash bare feet in the surf. No one has come prepared for this mislaid summer's day. They've brought no beach chairs or blankets. One young woman, having pushed up the legs of her long pants and the sleeves of her shirt, stretches out on her back in the bare sand. Kids build sand castles down near the water, delighted when a wave catches them off guard and soaks their clothes.

Nature's changes have been gentle this fall, not harsh or sudden, as often happens. It seems a metaphor for what we are experiencing personally — an easy transition in the seasons of our lives. There is serenity and happiness that neither of us ever experienced before.

Some people retire, sell their homes, move to Florida or Arizona or travel the world. But that is not even an option for us. The farm will never be sold, unless something unforeseen happens. I don't even think of it as mine to sell. Just as I inherited it and as my mother did before me, we, too, will pass it on to the children and grandchildren. But, that aside, I think this gradual break, a part-time change, will be more comfortable for us. The time is right to pull away, but not let go, of what we've held so dear.

When my parents were still alive, and later when Jack's mother — who outlived his father by 20 years — was in assisted living at Keswick, we needed to be close by. When the grandchildren were small, it was a joy to help care for them. They're almost all teen-agers now and will become more and more absorbed by their own interests, ambitions and dreams, as they go off to college and establish careers. We must stand back and let go, yet stay close, as friends as well as grandparents, to these burgeoning adults. And friends don't have to see each other every day for the relationship to be important or special.

I always lived on the same property with my mother and father, just as my daughters and their families do with me. Though I was busy with my television career as my mother and father were busy with their lives, when I was home, they were just a few steps away and I could see them every day if I chose to do that. However, it was when my mother and father were away, traveling, that I gained a better understanding of who they were as people.

Mother wrote me long, chatty letters that revealed touching insight into their personalities, their likes and dislikes and their relationship with each other, primarily how deeply my mother loved and admired my father.

My father was very handsome. When he was young and his hair and mustache were dark, people often said he looked like Clark Gable. As he grew older, his hair and mustache turned a silky white, making his handsome face look even more distinguished. He loved fine clothes, and he used to order custom-made raw silk sport coats from Hong Kong in many colors — beige, gold, robin's egg blue. He also had dozens of pairs of slacks, some of which he had never worn when he died. His ties were bold and bright.

My mother also bought silk dresses and suits from the same custom house, but not as many. Her blond beauty and gentle charm had captivated my father, but as she grew older, she stopped thinking of herself as pretty and no longer wanted or needed to draw attention to herself with fashion. But she never tired of watching my father dress up, and reveled in his attractiveness. She once wrote me from a cruise they were on: "Your father is the handsomest man in the dining room. Every night, he wears a different outfit. The people at our table can't wait for dinner to see what he'll be wearing."

In the era of women's liberation, when I, like so many other young women, was struggling to establish an identity for myself — outside the one as wife and mother — my mother's relationship with my father seemed subservient, yet it helped provide a balanced perspective. The devotion I saw, as well as the things she wrote to me, helped me understand that a woman such as she, with a college degree, who had been a teacher and independent before marriage, might choose to devote her life to her husband and family, not because she felt bound to do so, but because she wanted to. There was joy in the commitment she'd made and honor in the choice.

Many times, her letters just made me smile and provided me with a new awareness of her character and sense of humor. My mother was a very unselfish woman, and I always thought she put everyone's

Change

wishes before her own — even strangers'. At least that's what I thought until I got a very long letter written from the deck chair of another cruise ship they were on. The letter was several pages, front and back. It ended with: "I've been rambling on about all this because I'd rather write to you than talk to the annoying woman who's sitting next to me. I've been hoping that if I didn't pay any attention to her, she'd leave."

I was reflecting on my mother's letters in thinking about staying close to our children and grandchildren while living away. Jack will always be close to his son. They have long, extensive and now expensive phone conversations. Their conversations are worth whatever they cost. And when we're home, Jack makes the time and effort to drive to Washington to see him. Christopher may soon be moving to California, and then, I suspect, we'll do something we've been putting off for some time — we'll buy a computer so that they can exchange e-mail. And we'll start accumulating frequent-flyer miles at a much faster rate.

My daughters and I have not been as successful as Jack and his son. We live close, but everybody's just so busy: jobs, Scouts, Little League games. It seems one of us, or all of us, is always in a car, but rarely with each other. Perhaps when they visit us at the beach we can have some "quality time." O'Donnell, her husband, Steve, and their four children are coming for Thanksgiving, and Marjorie and her boys will be here for Christmas. Another change — a breaking of tradition and a chance perhaps to achieve growth from the difference.

It was after O'Donnell's 40th birthday dinner that I thought about writing letters, inspired by those my mother had written to me. At that dinner, I had asked everyone there, including the grandchildren, to help me capture the occasion on film. I passed my camera around and said, "Take the shot that you think best captures the mood of the party." "You mean the Kodak moment," my grandson Brian corrected. The picture taking not only added a note of fun to the party, but the photos were also very creative. We got the normal group shots and the gift-opening shots, but we also got the owners of the restaurant, Rudi Paul and Rudy Speckamp, the waitress, the chandelier and a close-up of the dinner roll that was served.

When Jack and I got back to the beach, I had the film processed and decided to send each grandchild one of the photos that he or she had taken. And I would send it with a long, chatty letter. But not too long

— I did want the children to read them.

In each of the letters, I told the children how proud Jack and I are of them, which we are. They are wonderful kids, and we not only feel blessed, but we also truly enjoy their company. I explained some particular points of pride we have in each one and highlighted individual characteristics that make each child different and why we find these characteristics pleasing. I refrained from talking about areas that might need improving. They have parents to do that. Besides, as they would say, "Been there, done that." Living so close and being a part of their lives since they were born, we've done our share of correcting. And that won't stop, because whether they heed your advice or not, you can't watch children you love head down a troublesome path and not try to keep them from harm. But that is, and always has been, primarily their parents' role.

Away from them now, for weeks at a time, we miss them. But I plan on using this time of not knowing about or having to deal with their daily problems to focus on the unique gifts of each grandchild and help make them aware of these attributes. Each of us values, and strives to build on, those assets that make us appreciated and loved. So, my letters to our grandchildren focused on the various positive traits they've exhibited: responsibility, good humor, kindness to animals as well as people, being conversational, with wide interests, being gracious, generous and showing common sense.

To one child, who is teased about not being as smart as the others, I wrote, "When my brother and I were growing up, people used to say I was lucky that I inherited my parents' good looks, because my brother got all the brains in the family. As a result, as a young woman, I tried to use what I thought was my one and only asset to establish a career. I became a model and got into television doing commercials. But," I went on in the letter to my grandson, "as you know, I've since been able to accomplish almost everything I wanted. I've been a television reporter, written several books, become a successful businesswoman and taught several college courses. I learned that it's not just how smart you are, but how determined you are and how hard you're willing to work to make your dreams come true."

Actually, this boy is as intelligent as the others, just not as studious. Clearly, he prefers to use his quick wit and charm to get laughs. My son was the same way, often struggling in school. But eventually he realized that he was as intelligent as I always told him he was, and then he excelled. Labeling children, even in apparent jest, as inferior in some way is dangerous. If you make a child believe that you expect little from him or her, that's usually what you'll get. But setting unreasonable expectations or demands is also potentially damaging. Not every child can be an "A" student any more than every kid who tries out for some sport will make the first string.

Love and common sense are always good guides, and getting a second opinion from a professional can be as beneficial in parenting as it is in health care.

The brains and beauty characterizations of my brother and me were also unfair to him. He is brilliant, but he is also attractive — tall, thin, with blond hair and blue eyes. I had teen-age girl friends who thought he was "really cute." But he never believed he was. And I wasn't a "dumb blonde." I did well in school, but it took me years before I believed in my intelligence. Before I did, I was constantly looking for reassurance that I was still attractive, because I feared that when I lost my looks, I would have nothing else to offer. The best part of my life has been discovering the rest of me and realizing the rewards of life beyond physical attractiveness and youth.

Perhaps I can help my grandchildren understand that labels, especially those attached to us by other people, can be extremely limiting and harmful if we believe them. I hope Jack and I can help the children understand and believe that they alone can determine the potential of their lives and not allow others, who might be too quick to judge, to cause them to give up on themselves.

Now that I've found the creative me and become more self-confident and independent, Jack says that the other men in my life got the best part of me — the young, attractive one, eager to please and be whatever they wanted me to be. He's kidding. I think. But guess what? It doesn't matter; I would never trade what I am now.

Of course, I'm kidding. Besides she's still beautiful,

and of course does whatever I tell her. Seriously, I knew and worked with that younger Susan, and, although I liked her, I had no desire to date her. Of course, she felt the same way about me. But that's another story. Back then, she seemed shallow, primarily because management (all men) only allowed her to do "fluff" stories in which she could flash her beautiful smile. Despite that perpetual smile, Susan chafed under those restrictions, but I hadn't bothered to really get to know her. When she left Channel 2 (to take on a less-demanding job and to try to save a failing marriage), it was the day my son was born, Oct. 23, 1970 — and I was glad she would no longer be part of the newscast. I said to some of my colleagues that now we could go back to doing real news. But when she returned, a year later, it was with the understanding, prompted by Susan's insistence, that she be allowed to cover every kind of news story.

She eagerly sought advice from me and others and learned so much so fast that soon I was asking her for advice. Grudgingly, I accepted the fact that she had progressed beyond me and was simply the best all-around reporter at the station — able to deliver hard-hitting investigative reports as well as moving vignettes on people and places. I was in awe. I still am. Our friendship grew, and, several years later, it grew into love.

Chapter 7

Opportunity
Of **Change**
The Cowboy

Change is inevitable; one needs only to walk the beach to realize that. Change rolls in with each rearranging wave, with each shift in the wind that moves the sand. What's important is how we handle change — fighting it or dealing with it. Certainly, to some degree, you can control change, as Jack and I are now, by initiating it.

Gil Breeding, a dear friend and one of my "significant others" because he helps us around the farm, will tell you he believes in that philosophy. But he will also tell you that sometimes you have to literally drive yourself out of a rut to make it happen. The rut is the easier path to follow. It takes imagination, determination, planning and timing to face the frontier of retirement.

Gil took early retirement at age 55, after working for 30 years as a forest ranger, a job he loved. It was being outdoors that led him to choose that line of work, and his passion for it made him an exceptionally good ranger. But, more and more, the increasing paperwork, computer technology and red tape were keeping him out of the field and in the office.

However, the final straw was the political correctness that had crept into our culture and our jobs. Gil said he felt as if Big Brother were watching, making him hesitant to do or say things that were an innate part of his fun-loving personality. It was turning this good-humored man, who loved to kid and share a joke, into a resentful, sour one. It

Opportunity Of Change

was affecting him physically, mentally and emotionally. So he retired and went into business for himself — farming, mowing, snow removal. He already had the equipment, and it kept him outdoors. And when he wasn't working, he'd ride on his horse through the woods he loved so much.

But it was a couple of years after retiring that Gil realized his life-long dream. If Gil were to tell you about it, he'd probably begin like this: "I've always been satisfied with my life — never envied other people, never wanted to be somebody I'm not. That is, with one exception. I always wanted to do what Gene Autry did in the movies: I wanted to ride the range; I wanted to be a cowboy."

Gil Breeding had never been west of Pennsylvania and yet he carried this dream from childhood, through his years in the Army, even after getting married and settling into his job as a ranger and taking care of his farm and later his elderly parents.

"I could never really shake it — I guess I never really tried," he said. "It didn't seem to get in my way — just kind of hung around to make those unbearable days bearable. I figure we all got to have dreams. What's life without dreams? Just one bill that needs paying after another. I just held on to the picture of me someday getting on my horse and following the setting sun, finding our way out onto the open space of America's plains and prairies."

He never did, never even took a short vacation out west. He was too busy being a good husband and neighbor (helping out whenever and wherever he was needed, as he helps me). Too busy being a good son and a foster dad. He and his wife, Janet, never had children of their own, but several times they took in other people's children to give them the love, discipline and lessons of life that these children hadn't gotten elsewhere. There was joy and reward in doing that, but also the pain of loss when the youngsters moved on or, in one case, a little girl whom they wanted to adopt, was taken away, to be adopted by a younger, more affluent couple.

Gil says of his dream, "I guess I never had a lot of time or reason to think of actually giving in to that idea of riding west. 'Foolishness,' my mother would have said."

In the spring of 1993, Gil's mother died at age 82. His father had died two years earlier. Only then did his dream begin to fill his thoughts more forcefully. Because then, for the first time, it actually

49

seemed possible. "The numbers fell into place," he says, meaning money and time. "They never had before." Something kept running through his mind, "I need to do this before it's too late — now — while I'm young enough and healthy enough to do it exactly the way I imagined."

There was only one person who could have stopped him, held him home — his wife, Janet — and he would have stayed without resentment. She was still working, and if he was to do this, he would have to do it alone. She had long known of his dream. "This is your chance," Janet said, without hesitation. "You may never get it again, and this way you will be experiencing precisely what you've always envisioned, doing it on your own."

Janet is a well-balanced woman. She is strong enough to be independent, but soft enough to need, want and accept help from her husband. With Gil away for several months, it would mean that, in addition to her job, she would also have to take on the farm and household chores that he usually did. She was more than willing to do it so that the man she loved and had been married to for 32 years could fulfill this lifelong ambition. And she was secure enough in her marriage to let her husband go off on his own for several months.

Gil believes that Janet's knowledge of horses might also have helped influence her acceptance. Like Gil, she's an accomplished horseback rider and has experienced the control a rider can have with a loose rein, if a horse has been properly trained. She also knows that if you let a good horse have its head, it'll always return to the barn, to the security and good care it's gotten there. Gil thinks she knew it would be the same with him. As he puts it, "What's good for a horse is good for a jackass."

And so, at age 57, Gil Breeding loaded his horse, Amigo, into the trailer behind his pickup truck and headed west. He had made no prior arrangements; he had no contacts, no list of names or places to stay. He was going to experience this adventure as it unfolded. His planning was not to plan, not to let a prearranged schedule get in the way of his freedom or the opportunities he might come across. Gil puts it this way, "If you don't know where you're going, you're never lost and you're never behind schedule."

As a result, his real-life experience became even better than the fantasy that he had cherished for all the previous decades. He stopped

Opportunity Of Change

and rode the plains, just pulled over to the side of the road, unloaded his horse and headed out for the horizon. A slow gallop became a race into the wind, as he urged Amigo to top speed — like the chase after the bad guys in every Gene Autry film. In one town, a rodeo was about to begin. Gil offered, and was given the chance, to ride in the opening parade around the arena. He rode carrying the Maryland flag.

In South Dakota, he hung out in small-town cafes and restaurants until this almost 60-year-old tenderfoot was hired on for a cattle drive — just like in the movies, except they didn't call him "kid." He rode the Badlands and the Black Hills. He made friends with ranchers and was invited into their homes. And he visited Gene Autry's ranch and museum. Gil unloaded Amigo and rode the ground that his hero had ridden, heard the sound of galloping hooves under him and felt the western wind whistle across his sun-dried face. He was the cowboy he always dreamed he could be.

When he came home, Gil was thinner than he'd been for 30 years. His muscles were tight and hard, and he never felt better in his life. Although he had known no one out west when he left home, he came back with a long list of new friends. These were people he had worked with, stayed with, had a meal with, slept under the stars with. One was a stranger who had given Gil and Amigo shelter during a sudden and powerful storm.

One woman and her husband with whom he became particularly close operated a sort of tepee bed and breakfast near Lusk, Wyo. They had a circle of tepees set up on bluffs overlooking the Cheyenne River, inviting travelers to sleep the night and have breakfast cooked over a campfire.

A year after Gil had met and stayed with them, the woman was diagnosed with breast cancer. The doctors out west suggested that she come east to a larger, more specialized medical facility to be treated. The Oncology Center at Johns Hopkins Hospital in Baltimore was chosen.

The woman, her husband and daughter came east. They stayed with Gil and Janet, and the friendships deepened. Gil drove them back and forth the 25 miles to the hospital, cheering them up when things looked grim, helping them celebrate when all went well. And while the woman was in the hospital recovering from having a breast removed, Gil served as tour guide for the husband and daughter as he drove them to Hopkins to visit.

The woman returns yearly for checkups and always stays with the Breedings. An alternative, such as a hotel near the hospital, has never been discussed.

By the time Janet Breeding retired in 1998, Gil had bought something she had always dreamed of having. It's a live-in horse van, one of those really big, luxurious trailers that has space for horses in the back, storage in the middle and lovely living and sleeping accommodations for humans up front. It's a big, shiny, silver-bullet type van that they call the "Horse Hilton."

Not long after Janet's retirement party, Gil loaded two horses into the "Horse Hilton," and off they went to ride the western range together. I wouldn't be surprised if someday they move out west; someday, when the time is right, when the numbers again fall into place.

Chapter 8

Exploring

Most often now, Jack and I walk or bicycle around the Rehoboth area. We use the car only for trips to the supermarket, the town of Lewes or beyond. At the end of our little beach street, which is a hodgepodge of broken macadam, small potholes and pockets of sand, turning left takes us to downtown Dewey Beach, to the right is the town of Rehoboth Beach. Going toward Dewey, at the intersection of Route 1, situated close to the bend in the road, is the Sunrise Restaurant. The orange neon OPEN sign brings in locals, off-season visitors and travelers from the highway.

It's a low, flat building with big windows. Inside, booths with lacquered wood tables hug the windowed walls. The rest of the eating area is filled with modular table units, with molded orange plastic chairs and black metal supports. The kitchen, in plain view through an open door, glass panels and a carry-out window, provides a comfortable, homey feel. Sunrise seems left over from the 1950s, offering nothing trendy, just fresh brewed coffee, great eggs, pancakes and home fries. The one difference is an extensive menu of omelettes. When Jack and I want to treat ourselves to breakfast out, we usually bike down there. Occasionally, we go the other way into Rehoboth to the equally good The Great American Diner, which also serves eggs Benedict. (However, we're told that this restaurant will be closed for the winter months and Sunrise stays open year-round.)

Exploring

The first weekend we were here, we went looking for bikes to rent and ended up at Atlantic Cycles, on Wilmington Avenue in Rehoboth Beach. The owner, a young man named Frank, said that in-season the going rate for renting a bike was $30 a week, but that at this time of year he could let us have them for $30 a month. But then he said, "Hey, I've got some used bikes in the basement that you could buy for about $25." We walked to the basement and I picked out a $25 bike that needed "a little work." Jack picked out a $40 bike that needed "going over." The man spent the rest of the day fixing them up, charging us nothing extra, and then when we picked them up later that day, he said, "At the end of your stay, if you don't want to haul them home, I'll buy them back from you."

"I think you just talked yourself out of making any money on this deal," I said gratefully, "but thanks, we sure appreciate it." That's how they are here, off-season, just glad to have you around.

I've been biking into Rehoboth everyday to go to the post office or photo shop (First State Photo processed most of the photographs in this book), or just to browse in the many shops that stay open all year. I love Quillen's Hardware, what a wonderful variety store. Forget those big warehouse places on Route 1, Quillen's has what I need, and the people there not only tell me where it is located in the store, but someone's always available to show me and talk to me in a neighborly way while doing it. "What are you and Jack doing now?" people in the store ask, "Are you still on television?" At the big chain stores, all that seems to matter is whether the computer accepts your credit card. The Quillen's of America are disappearing, but while this one in Rehoboth still exists, I pedal to it and spend a pleasant few minutes of a day shopping for a piece of wire, a can of bicycle oil or a plastic tarp.

The book store is always a favorite stop. So far, I've bought three novels, including Tom Wolfe's new one, "A Man In Full," and four books on local interests. There are two book stores in Rehoboth, that stay open year-round. Our favorite has become Browseabout Books. It has a little cafe area with good coffee, pastries, magazines and a wide variety of out-of-town newspapers.

The owners, Barbara and Steve Crane, mean it when they say "Browseabout." They make you feel welcome to spend as much time and as little money as you like.

Often, I bike toward Rehoboth just to ride around Silver Lake and enjoy the view. Jack also jogs around the lake, and his first time out he came back all excited, "Did you see it? Did you see what is growing on the bank of the lake, near the side of the road?" I had seen it. There, in early October, in the middle of a mowed section of grass, stood a single black-eyed Susan. My son's flower. The flower he always picked for me. The one that appeared on his grave several months after he died. Now with that lone wildflower growing out-of-season, "off-season," on the bank of the beautiful, reflective body of water just west of the dunes, it was as if his spirit had followed us on this adventure — a sign to me that this was right.

Silver Lake and its birds provide a welcome distraction while jogging. On my first day out, as I run beside the lake, a flock of ducks paddles quickly but quietly away, creating myriad V-shaped wakes along the water's surface. Farther on, the leaders of another grouping of ducks loudly protest my intrusion, and, suddenly, they all rise in unison, the air filled with the thrumming of their wings. Having made their point, they quickly resettle only a few feet from their original position. As I round a curve of the lake, ducks perched on the shoreline stand their ground, but their eyes never leave me. The geese are oblivious, and although I pass close enough to a heron to touch it, it merely pauses in mid-stride — one leg hovering — as it watches me warily. Overhead, a flock of migrating Canada geese brakes its V formation, spreading out in single file. The undulating line they form takes on the appearance of a huge flying serpent.

I've discontinued my runs around Silver Lake, realizing that it's been selfish pleasure. Angel can't run with me there, except on a leash, because of traffic and her urge to chase the birds, and she's not good on a leash. So now I run on the beach, where Angel has the freedom to wander, sniff, greet other dogs and then run to catch up.

Silver Lake is the largest of two fresh-water ponds on either side of Rehoboth Beach. Silver Lake is the closest one to us, spanning the south-

Exploring

east edge of Rehoboth and a small section of Dewey.

This fresh-water lake is quite near the ocean, with only a relatively narrow strip of land and sand, a few hundred feet wide, separating them. Along the strip, there are now large, expensive houses, which have the advantage of an ocean view on one side and the lake on the other. At one time, however, there was just sand holding the two bodies of water apart.

Local history reveals that each fall in the 1800s, farmers dug a trench across the sand strip to drain the lake and harvest the fish, which they would salt away for winter. The trench would then be refilled with sand, allowing the lake to once again fill with fresh water. It is believed that this practice was originally learned from the Indians, who were the first to live in the area of Rehoboth.

Beneath the serene surface of Silver Lake runs a strong undercurrent of conflict. Although lovely homes surround the lake and private docks and gazebos have been built out on its shoreline, the ownership of Silver Lake is still being debated. It has repeatedly been argued in the courts, but so far without final resolution.

Many long-time property owners around the lake think their land extends, in a pie shape, to the center of the lake. There are public roads on the north and west shores, between the houses and the water's edge.

The homeowners there maintain the banks of the lake across the road from their properties. They've planted grass and keep it mowed: there are numerous "Private Property" and "No Trespassing" signs along the banks, in the pines and on the docks they've built.

The most recent court dispute involved keeping a walking path on the south shore open to the public, and the judge left it open. But the property owners, appalled, appealed.

(Shortly before this book was completed, the court ruled in favor of the property owners. Dewey Beach and a residents group, not wanting to spend any more money to continue the fight for access to the footpath, dropped the legal battle, making the south end of Silver Lake private — at least for now.)

If you ask the municipalities about ownership of Silver Lake, you'll get different answers. But the consensus is that the triad of Rehoboth Beach, Dewey Beach and Sussex County, Del., are the rightful joint owners. However, further questions indicate that no one has been designated the official owners or caretakers of what is called "a natural gem of the shore."

About 15 years ago, when residents around the lake complained that hunters were shooting the wild geese and ducks drawn to the lake, the Delaware Department of Natural Resources put up a sign declaring Silver Lake a waterfowl refuge. Whether the state had a right to do that or not is in question, but it worked, and the lake is now a safe harbor for the ducks, Canada geese, cranes, herons and, surprisingly, a nest of green and yellow parrots.

There are lots of stories about how these tropical birds came to be residents of non-tropical Rehoboth, but no one knows for sure. One account says that their ancestors, being brought into this country for sale in pet stores, escaped when a crate broke open at Kennedy Airport in New York. Then, according to this tale, as they flew down the coast, they spotted Rehoboth Beach and, like many humans and other creatures, decided this was a good place to settle.

My favorite story is that a widow, about to die herself, set her cherished pair of parrots free so that they could go on living in her beloved Rehoboth Beach, even if she could not.

But the most likely account is that a pair of parrots, being kept as pets here, escaped while their cage was being cleaned and were never recaptured.

Exploring

However they got here, the parrots have adapted well. They've now been here for many years, multiplying and building three nests. Jack and I have counted 14 outside one of the nests.

Author Jennifer Acherman, in her book "Notes From The Shore," writes that they are truly "parrots," but are officially called South American monk parakeets and are native to central Argentina. She writes that others of their species that also escaped also adapted well and now thrive in various locations. She says there are colonies of "monks" in the greater New York area and as far north as the Canadian border.

The Rehoboth Beach "monks" have built three nests: one, on a light pole, on the north side of Silver Lake, another in nearby pine trees and the third a few blocks away on St. Lawrence Street, also built on a light pole.

The nests look like large cocoons (or squirrel's nest, only bigger), perhaps two feet long and maybe three feet around. There are two openings near the bottom, but the rest is enclosed, giving protection from inclement weather.

The nests on the light poles have been artistically and wisely woven under a transformer box and around a street light, both of which are a source of some heat in the winter months.

Apparently, these parrots eat seeds from pine trees and sunflowers, as well as grass, corn and human offerings such as bread, cheese, suet and commercial bird seed. A Dewey Beach resident, whom I met near the Silver Lake nest, told me that the parrots visit his home in the summer, when the fruit on his peach trees gets ripe. He says it's a tossup which is the noisiest, the raucous cawing of the parrots or that of the young party people of Dewey Beach.

My son, Christopher, who had spent a couple of intemperate, but not altogether enjoyable weekends in Dewey Beach, was stunned when I told him that was where we were going to get away from it all. "Dad, do you have any idea what Dewey Beach is like?" he asked, and then proceeded to tell me. And, as if to emphasize my son's warning, The Sun ran a big front-page article, in the Sunday feature section, about Dewey Beach, describing how this little resort

Exploring

is transformed into the beach binge capital of the Delmarva coast. Young professionals, primarily from the Washington area, rent houses, 30 to 40 males and females in each, where they sleep, briefly, crammed together on floors as well as overflowing couches and beds. That's during the day. At night, they party — drink-until-you throw-up-then-drink-some-more partying.

After Susan and I visited "our" house, I assured my son that it was a safe distance from party central, but also that, off-season, Dewey Beach is a quiet and peaceful place.

In addition, officials here are reportedly making plans to reduce the "in-season" raucousness — of the people, not the parrots.

Chapter 9

Thanksgiving

We awake to the sound of rain. The flannel sheets we've just put on the bed feel snug and make it tempting to stay nestled here and delay getting up. I run my hand over the soft surface and press my cheek into the pillow. "Flowers," I say to Jack, "they'd be even nicer with big, bright flowers on them," referring to the bed linens.

"You and your flowers — a flower bed on flannels — that's what you want, isn't it?"

"Yeah! That's it, a soft comfortable flower bed — and I'd never get up."

"Ummm, I might consider that," he says. Jack hates flowered prints on anything — clothes, curtains, furniture and especially on sheets. We settled on a plaid, with colors that match the comforter already on the bed, which is a flower print.

Except for feeding Angel and taking her for a walk, there is no hurry to get out of bed. The kids aren't coming down until tomorrow. They are going to my daughter's in-laws today. It will just be the two of us, and Angel, for our Thanksgiving meal. Jack's hand finds mine. This will be a first for us, celebrating a holiday alone.

The big Thanksgiving family gatherings that my parents started have dwindled in size in recent years. My daughters have been going to "family on the other side." Last year, Jack's mother joined us, but now she's gone. The rest of his family lives out west. Usually,

Thanksgiving

Christopher, Jack's son, is here, but he, too, will soon have "other" family, and he is with them this year.

The change is not bad. I feel a sense of calm as I watch the white-capped gray waves roll in, leaving a line of almost weightless foam behind the ebb of the tide. The wind lifts the foam with ease and scatters bits across the sand. We feel no sadness being alone on this day of family reunions. We are thankful that our children are healthy and happy, their lives full; thankful that we have each other to enjoy this quiet time, to nourish ourselves with thought, reflection and to be enriched by the nature around us.

After so many years of work and struggle, this is our reward, ours to selfishly relish. We've frankly discussed the toll that age or illness will eventually take, wondering which of us will have to bear the burden alone. But to worry about that now would foolishly and needlessly dilute the richness of what we have at this time.

The sun breaks through the clouds, casting shimmers of light upon the dark ocean. Droplets on the dune grasses glimmer with the brightness of a prism. Another couple, walking along the beach, comes into view. They, too, seem content, happy to be sharing each other's company, not feeling lonely on this Thanksgiving Day.

The long holiday weekend that follows brings more sunshine and the warmth of family closeness, the excitement of children, our grandchildren, visiting a new place — a beach house at a new time of year, off-season. Emily, almost 16, and the only granddaughter, had hoped to bring a girlfriend to share the stay with someone other than "just family." It didn't work out. But Emily finds the beach, shopping, bike riding and the now customary exchange of sarcastic, but good-natured digs with Jack fun enough. For Brian and David, the soon-to-be 14-year-old twins, and 10-year-old Alex, it is a chance to play football on the beach with their dad and throw tennis balls in the ocean for Angel to retrieve. At home, the boys play Little League baseball, and, whereas I have trouble getting the ball far enough out to be any kind of challenge for Angel, the boys sail it out so far I'm afraid she won't make it back. Brian hurls one ball such a distance that even Angel loses sight of it. It's probably in England by now, and Angel might still be swimming after it if we hadn't called her back.

With only two bikes, I take each child out one at a time to show him or her around: Silver Lake, how to get into Rehoboth, to the convenience store in Dewey and of course, I take each one to see the parrots, repeating my spiel about what they are and how they might have gotten here. Once the children are familiar with the territory, they venture out together, two by two.

Friday night after dinner, under a clear sky of bright stars, we walk the beach to the boardwalk for the Christmas tree lighting ceremony in the center of Rehoboth. Arm in arm, led by a musician on stage, we sing Christmas songs, loudly, with great gusto and mostly off-key.

Hundreds, perhaps thousands, of children and adults have gathered for the event, which is scheduled for 7 p.m. By 7:20, people are getting restless. "Light the tree," shouts a good-natured young voice. It is one of ours, who then attracts glares, mostly from his parents.

The singer, on stage, pauses to announce that the tree will be lighted at exactly 7:27. Puzzled frowns appear on many faces, but then I notice a tall microwave rod lifting high into the air from atop a local TV news van, sitting off to the side of the stage. I point it out to Jack, who nods knowingly. Of course, that's the reason for the delay. The local news is on from 7 to 7:30. The station wants a "live shot" of the tree to light up the screen just at the end of the newscast. It wouldn't be dramatic enough to take the picture with the tree already lighted — it has to happen "live." And so the television producer or reporter, on location, will signal the event officials when to throw the switch. This isn't explained to the people in the square waiting, nor will it be explained to the viewers at home. As if by sheer good timing, the dark tree on the TV screen will suddenly come aglow with lights, just as the reporter gives the cue. We'd performed such magic ourselves, and now feel some shame, belatedly realizing how we had probably inconvenienced other earlier crowds.

For those gathered around the tree on this night, the lighting of the tree, when it finally occurs, is so surprising that some miss it. The singer is in the middle of a song; there is no countdown, no warning at all. So some people are turned away when suddenly the tree is ablaze with colored bulbs, and they miss seeing what they had waited so long for and would

Thanksgiving

have seen if they had stayed home and watched it on TV.

With teen-agers around, it is a busy three days: breakfast at home or at the Sunrise restaurant, shopping at the outlets and the specialty stores of Rehoboth, bicycling, beach ball, followed by carry-out pizza and pasta. Saturday ends with a night as warm as any summer evening and with the kids out in the sandy cove, lying on the lounge chairs, gazing up at the stars — so many more visible here than near the bright lights of metropolitan areas.

Unprompted, unassigned, one by one they come into the beach house with poems they have written, asking to use the word processors to type them out. Just when you think the children of today are too busy, too programmed, too computer-crazed to think about or feel the power of nature's beauty, they surprise you with poems.

Ten-year-old Alex ends his this way: "Nothing to see but the black sky. With the bright moon shining on me. The only thing I hear is the waves, crashing against the beach. Knowing the sound will stay in my head forever."

Brian begins his with: "As I sit on the beach and look at the stars, I wonder how far they really are. Are they really, really far away, or are they just across the bay."

From David: "Rough and grainy sand — meets the smooth and silky sea — Stars are bright; moon is too — It will not end."

And Emily concludes hers with: "It's now getting dark, Our day's almost done. I just can't believe, I had so much fun."

Does any grandparent need any more? This one doesn't.

To top off the weekend, on Sunday morning, my daughter, O'Donnell, and I go off biking — just the two of us. We ride into Rehoboth for coffee at Brew Ha Ha, sit at a table in the courtyard and talk, really talk, as adults, about adult things. The family visit, in new surroundings, provides many reasons to give thanks.

Chapter 10

December

Colored lights circle the shop windows and are draped along roof tops. White lights in the shapes of seahorses, mermaids, snowmen and Santa's sleigh adorn the median strip down Rehoboth Avenue. Red ribbons and bows on pine and holly hang in doorways. And on King Charles Street, at the corner of Newcastle, on the side lawn of Mayor Sam Cooper's house, a 60-foot Norway spruce shows off more than 4,000 multicolored lights. The tree is also easily seen from the boardwalk and, perhaps, even by the ships at sea. The Cooper family has been trimming this tree for more than 50 years.

The warmest fall in many years continues into December, with temperatures on many days hitting record highs. The Christmas decorations seem to clash with the roses and other flowers still blooming along the borders of green yards. On Dec. 5, the town of Lewes opens its doors to visitors for the annual holiday historic house tour and leaves them open because it's so warm. On a porch of one decorated house, a red-suited, white-bearded, bell-ringing Santa welcomes guests by saying, "Go on in, it's cool inside."

The town of Lewes dates back to 1631, when it was called "Zwaanendael," a Dutch word originally spelled with an S, and meaning valley of the swans. Swaanendael was an ill-fated Dutch settlement that was ultimately wiped out by the Siconese tribe of the Lenni Lenape Indians, following what now seems a relatively minor

December

incident — the theft of a settlement sign bearing the Dutch coat of arms. However, it so enraged the settlers that it led to a confrontation, which infuriated the formerly friendly Indians, causing them to massacre everyone in the settlement.

Eventually, the area was claimed by the British, and, when Delaware became part of the Pennsylvania land grant package to William Penn, it was he who gave it the Anglo-Saxon name of Lewes, in the county of Sussex.

For Lewes, there were two obvious growth spurts, separated by about 150 years. The houses built in the 1700s are simple, with clean lines that have worn well, weathering two centuries — houses such as the "Shepherd-Houston House" on Shipcarpenter Square. This is a wonderful example of a true center-hall Colonial, with much of the original woodwork — floors, moldings, chair rail and the fireplace wall. The back staircase, off the kitchen, remains exactly as it was built in 1780. Lewes is a treasure trove of 18th century houses.

But it is the larger Victorian houses, built in the late 1800s, during the railroad boom near the turn of the century, that are the showiest and draw the most attention.

These are houses with carved wooden porches, ornate trim and scrollwork — a decorative design that has come to be called "gingerbread." Many of the Lewes Victorians retain all their original porch work, restored and painted with period colors.

The Ross House, on Savannah Road, built in 1898 by breakwater diver John Ross, now sports colors of pale coral, seafoam blue and a darker aqua, perhaps the color of the ocean when Lewes was "Swaanendael." In recent years, Lewes has attracted residents who were not only interested in buying homes and living here, but also in renovating and restoring the houses with historic accuracy. The result is a visual treat for visitors, whether on a house tour or just driving through.

The Ross House is owned by Etta and Joe Kosaveach, who came down from Washington looking for the sanctity of a small town and the charm of the past. Joe was retired, and Etta was soon to be. They didn't think they would be able to afford anything in Lewes, which enjoyed an explosion of rediscovery and price in the early and mid-'90s. They looked at the town of Milton first, but then drove over to Lewes, and found just what they were looking for, within their price range.

The Ross House had been turned into a duplex by the previous owners and needed a lot of fixing up, all of which fit into the Kosaveaches' plan.

Joe's elderly mother was coming with them, and the duplex made it possible for all of them to have their own space. Or as Etta puts it, "My own kitchen. I loved my mother-in-law, but I don't like sharing my kitchen with anyone." Lewes was truly a haven for the elder Mrs. Kosaveach. She walked the streets alone, in safety, and made friends with shopkeepers and other townspeople who looked out for her. And the house is located across from the town park, where parades, ceremonies and other activities occur. She could sit on the porch, surrounded by all that antique "gingerbread," and watch life in a resurging waterfront town unfold, surrounded by people who had come to know her and care about her. Etta says, "Try finding that kind of situation in Washington or any big city these days."

In the spring of 1997, at age 92, Mrs. Kosaveach died, and thus began the 18-month renovation of the house to what it is today — a showplace that includes one of the finest private antique collections anywhere. Many of the items have already been designated to various museums, as outlined in Etta's and Joe's wills.

In talking about retirement life in Lewes, Etta says, "You can be as busy as you want to be or as lazy; it's your choice." She and her husband belong to a group associated with the Delaware Technical and Community College, called Adult-Plus, that organizes numerous trips and activities, such as excursions to New York to see shows. "And," says Etta, "there are endless opportunities to volunteer for such a wide range of interesting things you could never be bored here. If you are, it's your fault."

Many of the people I meet on the house tour, wearing committee member tags, tell me they are retired or about to be, and enjoying it more than they ever anticipated they would. One woman, serving as a tour guide, was originally from Baltimore, and she recognizes me from television.

She is a strikingly attractive woman, thin, stylish, looking years younger than the age she implies she must be. Her story is one I'm beginning to hear over and over again. "When my husband retired, we wanted a less stressful way of life. We used to vacation in Ocean City, but that's more transient than we wanted. We wanted something more year-round, so we settled on Rehoboth. We sold our home in

December

Baltimore and bought one here. My husband plays golf, and I do other things. I belong to several art leagues, I volunteer. I'm so busy, yet it's tranquil. I hardly know what's going on in the rest of the world. Are we at war?" she jokes.

I find out that her name is Faith Lord, and when I get back to the beach house, Jack says he thinks that he went to school with her husband, Don, at the University of Maryland. The world in retirement shrinks even more.

As with Faith Lord, the other year-round residents I'm meeting are involved in community events, such as the Halloween and Christmas activities, the annual Jazz Festival, and the first of what will become the annual Rehoboth Film Festival, which featured Baltimore filmmaker John Waters. There's a big commitment to charities and cultural functions, which serve as social outlets as well as civic undertakings, for all segments of the population, including retired people.

The locally published schedule of events, in both Rehoboth Beach and Lewes, is considered as much a social calendar as it is one of "things to do." For example, the people who worked on the house tour and the ones who attended came dressed up for the occasion.

They wore brightly colored Christmas sweaters, red blazers and suits. There was a variety of festive green and red plaid garments: skirts, slacks and at least one man's jacket. Other men dressed in tweed sport coats, and some women wore velvet.

Practically everywhere I go, except on the beach, the dress is smart and fashionable, though casual, but not the winter sweats I came prepared to wear and expected to see others wearing. Women take care with their hair and makeup, and many seem fit, indicating that diet and exercise are part of their routine. These are not only the young, working individuals, but also the older retired people I see. The people I'm meeting my age and older have not come here to go to seed, but to continue growing in the rich, relaxed soil of off-season years at the shore.

Chapter 11

Hometown Hero

Unsung heroes of an aging generation. You'll find them in almost every town, large or small, across America. The young are usually not aware of them, and often they are taken for granted by their contemporaries, perhaps because their heroics have faded like the flickering, old, black and white film clips of World War II or, worse, perhaps because we no longer care.

Eighty-two-year old John Brown patiently wraps strings of white Christmas lights around the bradford pear trees in the middle of Rehoboth Avenue. He wobbles, steadies himself, then stands erect, "This going around in circles is making me dizzy," he says with a smile.

He wears blue work pants and a khaki shirt suitable for his city job — taking care of 31 acres of parks in Rehoboth Beach. Over the work clothes, he has on a natty olive green Shetland sweater, topped off by a dapper Irish-style walking cap in the same shade of wool. His gray hair is cut close around his ears and neck. Suntanned skin loosely covers a square jaw and prominent nose. There are lines on his face, but not as many as you'd expect for his age and a life spent outdoors.

Aviator sunglasses add a dashing touch to this older version of what certainly must have been a handsome young man — likely head-turning handsome in the uniform of a tank commander of the 20th Armored Division, U.S. Army, under the command of Gen. George S. Patton.

"You served with Patton?" I ask impressed.

Hometown Hero

"Yeah, it was rough," he says matter-of-factly. And then, with a laugh, he adds, "Old 'Blood and Guts' — our blood and his guts."

John Brown grew up on a farm in the Milford area of Delaware, one of five children, and he's never known what it is not to work. He farmed and operated a country store until he was drafted in 1942, at the age of 24. For the next four years, he was in the thick of battle, entering at Le Havre, France, and ending in Munich with the takeover of Hitler's SS Center. "We were on our way to Japan when they dropped the bomb," he says without malice, but with a hint of the jubilance he must have felt at the end of the war.

Talking to John Brown about fighting in World War II makes me think about the war effort on the homefront that I've been reading about — specifically in Rehoboth Beach and all along the coast, from the mouth of the Delaware Bay down into Maryland and the Chesapeake Bay. As John Brown and thousands of other young American men were going overseas, German U-boats were coming this way to destroy U.S. merchant ships. They also posed the threat of putting enemy agents ashore.

The watch towers, erected then, remain along the beaches now and have become tourist attractions, lingering symbols of just how close the war came to the East Coast.

Rehoboth residents of that era can remember standing on the boardwalk, watching oil tankers and other commercial vessels burning offshore after being torpedoed by Nazi subs.

During the years of surveillance, in an effort to give the merchant ships some air cover protection, the Civil Air Patrol was established. Part of what the civilian pilots did was to spot German submarines and alert the Dover Army Air Base to their location.

John Brown pays homage to those men by pointing out to me that there is a memorial up near the boardwalk, in the bandstand park, which commemorates the lives lost in that effort. That monument stands with two others, paying tribute to the hometown soldiers killed overseas, during World War II, as well as in the other 20th century wars.

John wraps another tree with lights. He seems more eager to talk about his homecoming than the battles fought and his friends that died.

"I wasn't home two days when the gas company offered me a job. I said, 'I just got home. I was thinking maybe I'd take two weeks off.' They said, 'No, we need you now — take two days off and come to work.' So I did. Probably wouldn't know what to do with myself if I didn't have work to do. I'm sure if I stopped working, I'd fall apart in 30 days."

A heart attack six years ago put him in the Salisbury Hospital for a triple bypass operation and a heart-valve replacement. That didn't slow John for very long. He was soon back to work. His doctor now says, "Keep on doing whatever it is you do, because you're doing great."

The secret for John Brown is work, and always has been. After his employment with the Shore Gas Company, he took a job with Wilson Plumbing & Heating. Later, he operated his own propane gas business, Mobile Flame, and now he's under contract to the city of Rehoboth Beach to take care of the parks.

John has never considered retirement. His wife, Ellen did in 1992, from her bank job, but she quickly went back to work, part-time, for the Chamber of Commerce. They both feel more content working, especially the work they are now doing, work that improves the quality of life in their community.

John mows grass, trims bushes and even feeds the domestic ducks on Lake Gerar. Unlike the wild ducks, the white Muscovy ducks can't fly great distances to corn fields and marshes to feed on their own. So, each day, John brings them food. Then, standing guard, he shoos away the more aggressive wild ducks, which outnumber the tame ones and would gobble up all the grain if John weren't there.

John Brown has a good heart, patched up or not. He's long been committed to doing volunteer work, primarily with the Rehoboth Aid Services, a charity that helps the poor with food and financial emergencies.

In December, John Brown's duties include decorating the town with strings of Christmas lights. And for more than 20 years, he has overseen creating and placing the floating Christmas trees in Lake Gerar and Silver Lake.

"I love it. I just love every bit of it," he says with enthusiasm. Glancing at me out of the side of his sunglasses, there's a sparkle in his eye, joy in his voice. It's much more than pride in what he's done; he also enjoys looking at the lights and decorations, being around them, as much as other residents and visitors do.

The floating trees are not really trees. They are made by attaching clipped branches of spruce and fir onto a frame that's shaped like a tree. Many of the pieces of evergreen used for this are those John has trimmed from trees in the parks. Some are donated by other Rehoboth

Hometown Hero

residents, who also like being involved with the unique decorations. Three such trees are placed in Silver Lake and two in Lake Gerar.

The trees, strung with colored lights, are floated on two pieces of Styrofoam, anchored and illuminated by underwater electric lines that are plugged into outlets near the edge of the lake. A timer is attached to turn them on after dark. The trees' lights, reflected on the lake's dark surface, create a shimmering mirrored image. The water defuses and transforms them into rippling, stained-glass Christmas trees.

Jack and I drive around Silver Lake to admire the trees on our way to the Christmas parade that is held in the center of town in the middle of December.

Parades are big on the shore. Twenty thousand people attended Rehoboth's Halloween parade for the Sea Witch Festival. But the Christmas parades, throughout the Delmarva region, are the most popular. They work their way up the coast. This year, they started in Berlin, Md., moved on to Ocean City, then up to Lewes, and now back down to Rehoboth.

They say, "Everybody loves a parade." Well, not everybody. And some, such as Jack, have to be in the right mood. On this evening, Jack is, as they also say, "settled in" — reading a really good book, and he has just opened a good bottle of wine. He's adamant, "I'm not going!"

I go. Rehoboth is as crowded as on a summer weekend, except everyone is wearing heavy winter coats, with scarves and even blankets draped over their heads. However, they are still festive. Many, who have come early to get a parking spot along the parade route, are having tailgate parties, although many others remain huddled in their cars. I overhear one woman telling her grandson, "It would be really cold if there were a wind coming off the ocean. But there's not," she explains reassuringly, "so it's not cold." The boy looks at her, puzzled, and says, "Then how come I feel so cold?" "It's your imagination," she replies patiently, "you know what a wonderful imagination you have."

On this night, downtown Rehoboth Beach is an interesting and amusing mix of beach resort and

North Pole: people wearing reindeer antler hats and Santa mittens while buying Dolle's saltwater taffy on the boardwalk; sitting in beach chairs and watching Christmas parade floats passing places with names such as "The Loungin' Lizard," "Beach Graphics" and "Quiet Storm."

There is a warm, hometown feeling on this chilly night, and that's what I love about parades. Much of what is right with our world is marching down Rehoboth Avenue — Brownies dressed like Christmas trees, Boy Scouts as snowmen; dogs that make therapy visits to nursing homes trot by with antlers on and with their costumed owners in tow.

The Lion's Clubs of Rehoboth and Dewey Beach, which support so many worthwhile projects and charities, are recognized with loud applause.

And there is the young man from the bike store, Frank of Atlantic Cycles, with some of the 20 kids he sponsors in bicycle moto-cross racing — teens and pre-teens being guided into a healthy outlet for their adolescent energy.

And in an antique car, rolling past the reviewing stand, is John Brown. He'd told me he'd be at the parade, but he hadn't told me he'd be in it. "Sure, I'll be up there," he said, "It's part of my job — in case someone gets tangled up in all these electric wires, trips over them and pulls the plugs. We wouldn't want the lights to go out."

The announcer introduces him over the loud speaker. "Going past the reviewing stand now is John Brown, the man responsible for all the beautiful lights around Rehoboth Beach and for many other good things that happen here." John waves to the crowd, as a loud cheer envelops him. The applause follows him along the entire parade route.

John Brown is a hometown hero, and the people here do care, but, it seems, not for what he did in World War II, as heroic as that was. He is loved and respected for what he does now, every day. And that's fine with him. It is the way he wants to live his life. He is too busy to look back. There's much too much to do up ahead to linger in the past.

Chapter 12

Winter
Warmth

December 21. The weather seems as reluctant as I to acknowledge winter or that Christmas is near. Jack joins me on the porch for sunrise. He looks so relaxed, his expression soft with a gentle smile and a tender look about his eyes. He seems to be savoring every moment. "Look at this," he says, taking my hand, "the first day of winter — do you believe it? Look at that sunrise."

"Write it down!" I say, and he does.

The first day of winter and we're sitting on the porch, comfortably warm in just sweat shirts. Sipping coffee, we watch the sun rise, slowly peeking out from behind the blue haze covering the horizon, then glowing fully for only a minute before it is partially hidden again by the ribboned cloud cover, which seemingly twists and bends the sun into a glowing abstraction.

I look forward to each morning now with the same eager anticipation I felt during most of my working days in television. That excitement dwindled during my final years in the business, when such slogans as "News You Can Use" translated into such so-called news stories as which razors women should shave

Winter Warmth

their legs with, demonstrated by shapely models so men would also watch. No, I'm not being critical just because I wasn't assigned to do that story.

In this new "stop and smell the roses and enjoy the sunrises" phase of my life, my enthusiasm for each day has returned. I delay going to bed, and I can't wait to get up. "What are you doing these days?" friends ask. I answer, "More of everything I always did, except work." Think of all the things you want to do, enjoy doing, but put off because you just don't have the time. In all honesty, in retirement, there still isn't enough time. But there is a lot more of it.

The only thing I feared I'd miss when I stopped working was the camaraderie and laughter. Although news standards may have slipped, most of the people in TV news are interesting and fun, and I'd established relationships in which bantering back and forth provided a lot of laughter every day. But Susan and I have always had that same bantering relationship — we used to break each other up even during newscasts — and now we have time to laugh a lot together, and with our friends, old and new. So the secret of planning a happy retirement: marry someone you really like, as well as love. For me, love, friendship and laughter are the greatest pleasures of life. (Sex is included under love and friendship. Sex is also, as you may have noticed, the source of a lot of laughter.)

As I look at the beautiful sunrise, I think, "If I were still working, right now I'd be running to my car to begin that hour-plus commute to D.C. — facing traffic jams second only to Los Angeles — and worrying about being hit by another deer." My car was rammed twice by deer on Georgia Avenue. The last time, last year, caused more than $2,000 in damages. The only good part was that I didn't have to pay a deductible, because insurance companies deem a collision with an animal to be an act of God. As an act of

Winter Warmth

God, I'll take a sunrise any day.
I drink the rest of my coffee — sigh a contented sigh
— get up and make the short trip from the porch to
the kitchen to refill my cup.

It feels so-o-o good to have this Jack back in my life. So I prod him, or perhaps shame him, into writing with me about our off-season experience, and, in a way, re-establish what we had when we anchored a newscast together.

On the Noon News, I loosened him up. I plotted, planned and schemed continuously about what I could say on live television that would bring about the spontaneous release of the warmth and humor that lay beneath the controlled surface of this no-nonsense, "hard news" man.

By breaking him up at times when it was appropriate, I allowed the viewers to see his fun-loving side, his wit and charm and the infectious laugh that caused me to fall in love with him.

When people say to me, "How's retirement going? Are you sick of each other yet?" I explain that the hard part of our marriage was when Jack went back to work in television in Washington and I stayed home. During the 20 years we worked together at Channel 2, we'd spent a good part of each day together. For the first 10 years, we were colleagues and friends, and then we fell in love and married. The next 10 years, we lived together, worked together, vacationed together, anchored a newscast together and even went out on strike together. Then came the years he worked in Washington and I saw very little of him. "No," I say to those who ask, "we're not sick of each other yet. We're just getting back to where we were before the job in D.C. came between us."

I know what we have is extraordinary. But there are rough spots in every relationship, and retirement can cause added strains. The old saying, "For better or worse, but not for lunch," can become a real issue and not just a cute adage.

Recently, I was talking to a woman in a doctor's office, the receptionist/assistant, who asked what Jack and I were doing now. The conversation evolved to the changes created by retirement and how individual couples handle them. I tossed out the "not for lunch," quote and she responded with a forced and poignant little laugh revealing that her experience had not been a humorous one. She said, "My husband was an insurance salesman, so he worked odd hours — nights, weekends, whenever it was convenient for a client to see him. When the children were little, my husband made a habit of always coming home for lunch, so that he and the children could count on having that time together, every day. It was sacred time to him; he was always there for lunch, without fail." She sighed, and went on.

"Even after the children were all in school, he continued the practice. It then became our time. When the children married and left home, I started working with my husband in his business, and we were always together, including for lunch. Then came retirement and I started getting involved in other things, community work and going shopping with friends. But my husband was content to become less active, and he still counted on our continuing the lunch tradition. He just expected that I would be there. We didn't talk about it, he'd just say, when I left the house, 'See you for lunch.' I found myself looking at my watch all the time, cutting short shopping trips, not ever having lunch with the "girls;" leaving meetings early. Finally, I said to my husband, 'Could we do lunch less often, not every day? We'll make a date. It'll be special, not just expected."

Her eyes misted in remembrance, "He was hurt, really hurt — but we adjusted, and I think it was good for him. He got involved in other things, such as volunteer work, at lunch time."

Her husband is no longer alive, and she now works full-time. I'm sure she misses those lunches, but at the time she needed a change. And, though wistful, she now seems reconciled that she made the right decision then.

We can't know the future, so we must make choices based on things as they exist. All of us would have done something different, often many things, if we had known how things would turn out.

I think Jack and I are finding retirement so comfortable, whether it's here at the beach or back on the farm, because we don't try to do everything together. Jack rises before I do, and usually we eat different things at different times for both breakfast and lunch. We fix it for ourselves or eat while we're out doing things. We rarely grocery shop together, but do confer on what we need. Our one constant, with rare exception, is that we always have dinner together, and, whether we eat in or out, it's likely to be the high point of our day.

Winter Warmth

Some of our younger friends, trying to get a perspective on what lies ahead for them and not sure how they'll handle life without the structure of a job and faced with "all day" spouse association, say, "Describe a typical day."

Our daily schedules differ. Jack might be out all day, running errands, working out at the gym or going to various libraries to do research. I might be working in the office, in our home, or both of us might be at home working separately. We both might be out, or we might spend the entire day working together, writing or talking.

The combinations are many. We have separate but close lives — two uniquely individual people who enjoy being around one another, working together and sharing household duties, but not joined at the hip by retirement. That, for us, would be suffocating, uncomfortable and awkward.

The division of housework has just sort of evolved over the years. When Jack was still working in television, he hired a cleaning service to come in every two weeks. I complained, "I'm home, I can do it. We shouldn't spend the money."

"Yeah," he said, "you can, but you won't." Jack likes a very clean house and sanitary kitchen. I like it neat, but I'm not as exacting as Jack. So I half-heartedly let other women come into our home and rearrange my things to satisfy him. I am someone who has a place for everything, and I like them in those places, not off to the other side of the table or one shelf down.

With retirement, we've cut the cleaning service back to once a month, and I have to admit that it is nice to get everything thoroughly cleaned each month after not entirely successful attempts to keep it that way from the last visit.

Here at the beach, we sweep up everyday — the sand and Angel hair — vacuum the rugs, take out the trash. We take turns — whoever gets to it first. Usually, that's Jack. I cook dinner, a job we shared until Jack started working in Washington. But after letting him prepare just one dinner in our "new life" — a delicious spaghetti carbonara — I realized I didn't want to relinquish that duty, because I truly enjoy cooking. It brings my day to a satisfying end.

I also enjoy cooking. To me, it's as creative as any other art, and I will eventually reclaim my share of the kitchen. But, during the transitional period, I will magnanimously agree to be catered to at the dinner table by my wife, the chef. But, after the meal, I draw the line. I clean up.

I want to do my share. Although I'd been married before, when I married Susan, I had been a bachelor for a long time and was used to taking care of myself. I'm rather uncomfortable with doting, subservient women and with men who need such women. Susan is the sort of strong, independent, intelligent, fun-loving woman to whom I've usually been attracted. She constantly surprises, amuses and challenges me. I married her because I'd rather be with her than anyone else, and such things as her culinary skills were never an issue, but a delightful bonus. However, I am convinced that men and women are different, although not quite as different as Venus and Mars. Susan is, as are most women I've known, more nurturing than most men — softer, warmer, more caring and gentle. And, being as self-centered as any man, I must admit I enjoy most of Susan's attempts to take care of me. Most, but not all.

Which brings me to the laundry room. As with the kitchen, it is a home front where battles may occur. So Jack and I usually take care of our own laundry.

It was a wonderfully warm November day. I was sitting out on the lounge chair, in our sandy cove, enjoying the afternoon sun. Never had I felt so blessed. The porch door opened and out stepped the marvelous man with whom I was sharing this bliss. But he didn't look blissful. "Did you wash my black turtleneck?" he growled. My eyes followed his to the object in his hands. He held it out to make sure I got a good look.

He was holding a very small black turtleneck shirt, a miniature version of a Brooks Brothers style that had been discontinued, his favorite sweater, which could not be replaced, the one with the label that reads: 100 percent wool — dry clean only. Feeling particularly loving and helpful that morning, I'd gathered up Jack's laundry to do it for him. Without thinking, I apparently shoved the black sweater into the pile

Winter Warmth

with the black sweat pants and other dark-colored "washables."

Staring at Jack holding his favorite sweater, which now might, might, fit Angel or one of our younger grandchildren, my face grew hot and I swallowed before trying to speak. Nothing came out, so I nodded my head, admitting that I must have washed it. I didn't think he was in the mood for me to point to Angel.

Between bursts of swearing, he said, "I've asked you to PLEASE LET ME DO MY OWN LAUNDRY. My very favorite sweater — ever." Jack turned and stomped into the house. I could see him pacing and muttering to himself. I stayed on the lounge chair knowing there wasn't anything I could do now. I'd wait for him to cool down, go in, apologize and tell him that somehow, somewhere, I'd find him another one. (Which I haven't been able to do so far.) The good thing about Jack is that when he gets upset, he erupts and then it's over. Most often, it's himself he gets angry with. But not this time.

When I finally went in to apologize and to admit how stupid it was to have not even looked at the label on the sweater before tossing it in with the rest of the clothes, he said he was sorry for getting so upset. He knew I hadn't meant to do it; he'd just felt such a surge of frustration when he was taking the clothes out of the dryer and saw it.

"By the way," I said, "just for the record, it wasn't washing your sweater that shrank it. It was the hot dryer that did it."

He glared at me, "Oh," he said, "so it was the dryer's fault."

"Well, sort of," I said, with a hopeful smile.

"Why don't you just say, the devil made me do it?" he said.

"Or Angel," I said, "either one works for me."

We both laughed.

Chapter 13

White Christmas

December 23. As night settles in, a light, non-threatening snow begins to fall. It gently covers the sand and boardwalk in front of the beach house and clings to the pines and bushes. A breeze sweeps the snow into piles at the base of the dunes and sifts it through the frames of the lounge chairs. Just today I had put the cushions away. It is still snowing when we go to bed.

Christmas Eve. The day before Christmas dawns white, but there is now more ice than snow. Angel eagerly runs outside and immediately slides off our little boardwalk, onto the sand, which is also frozen over. She looks around, bewildered, as if caught in a dog's version of the Twilight Zone. Deciding quickly to hold it all in, she runs back inside.

But it is beautiful: the steel gray sky, the darker gray of the ocean and the rolling line of white-capped waves. An icy coating accents the dark brown planking of the boardwalk and the wood railing by the steps over the dunes. Framing the brown is the tall, beige beach grass, also fringed with ice, gracefully bowing under its weight. Our cove is a wavy patchwork of indented sand and ice.

White Christmas

I feel as excited as when I was a child on Christmas morning, with the surprises of presents and a decorated tree. I grab my camera and run outside without bothering to put on a coat or gloves, spurred impulsively to take it all in before it changes, perhaps melts away. Which present to open first, which shot will be best? Heeding Jack's warning, "Be careful. Everything's coated with ice," I test the footing, sliding slowly across the boardwalk, inching along to the frozen railing. The cold stings my hand as I grip the railing tightly to keep from slipping on the steep, ice-covered steps to the beach. Walking is difficult. With each step, I must kick through the ice to the frozen sand or else I will fall. Angel knew better; animals often do. As I focus and snap each beautiful scene, I wonder if the photographs will accurately portray what I see. The icy serenity of the empty beach, the crystal coating of the dunes, the warmth and comfort of the lights shining through the windows of the beach house. What an exquisite, priceless gift nature has provided on this Christmas Eve.

I guess I've never outgrown the simple pleasure of stomping around in the first snowfall of the year, forging through the unmarked coating and savoring the cold air as it colors my cheeks and nose. Even now, with the increased stiffness and occasional pain of arthritic knees, I'm unable to resist the temptation to play in newly fallen snow. And so I bundle up and walk the beach to the Rehoboth Boardwalk.

I never shared Susan's enthusiasm for this kind of weather. But now, savoring the silent beauty of falling snow has brought back the delight I experienced as a child whenever it snowed. It is a delight I re-experienced, all too briefly, through the eyes of my son, who magically transformed me into a playmate instead of a father as we sledded, threw snowballs, built snowmen and made snow angels. It is easy to overlook the beauty and fun of snow when you're stuck among frustrated, tire-spinning commuters, as I was for so many years. And, as a reporter, I hated being sent out into every snowstorm to do the same stories, over and over again, about how to cope with what weather forecasters characterize as something akin to Armageddon. But now

White Christmas

there is time to enjoy snow again. Another reason why retirement makes so many of us feel young again.

A mixture of sleet and snow begins to fall, blowing strongly out of the north, the direction in which I'm walking. I tuck in my chin and pull my hat down as snugly as I can.

By the time I reach the boardwalk, snow alone is falling, and it quickly piles up over the ice, making the footing more secure. I pull back my hat to take in the whitening world of the seashore. I've never seen a snow-covered beach before. The dunes now appear to be mounds of snow, growing grasses made of ice.

I'm all alone; there are no footprints on these boards striped with white. Icicles hang from the street signs at every crossroad — Prospect, Queen, Newcastle, Philadelphia. The shops, game pavilions, pizza places are boarded up. It is a black and white world, abandoned by people and the multicolors of summer. And then, like Dorothy stepping into Oz, I reach Rehoboth Avenue and enter the Technicolor world of Christmas on Main Street America. Colored lights sparkle on storefronts and in shop windows. Christmas music blares from loudspeakers on light poles and mingles with the laughter of last-minute shoppers. From the open window of Dolle's, a clerk selling saltwater taffy and caramel corn calls out, "Merry Christmas." A man of good will, whether I buy his confections or not. He is satisfied by my smile and wave. My mood soars in this setting, where strangers meet — briefly exchanging smiles and good wishes — all happy just to be sharing the spirit of the season and the Christmas Eve snow.

By early afternoon, the iced dune grass and bushes refract sunlight into the colors of the rainbow — small beads of red, orange, yellow, blue, green and violet, like small Christmas tree lights. It occurs to me that this may be how the idea of tree lights came about. The beach is completely white, except for the narrow strip of sand washed by the waves. On the beach, a rare sight: a young boy sledding. He slides down a snow-covered sand dune, using a kitchen tray as a sled. It recalls images from my days at the University of Maryland, when those of us who worked in the dining hall to pay for room and

*board also "borrowed" trays to go sledding on the hills
of College Park. Farther up the beach, in Rehoboth, children are standing in line outside a small shack, waiting
for a "photo op" with Santa Claus and to make sure
they're on his twice-checked list.*

With visions of iced beach plums dancing in our heads — and sure
that Santa can bring nothing more spectacular than Mother Nature's
gift — we sleep soundly.

*Christmas Day. A white Christmas in this the warmest
year on record. With Susan still snug in our bed, I sit
alone on the porch, sipping coffee and petting Angel,
who sits beside me. Only the low rumble of the ocean
can be heard in the frozen stillness. The landscape is
barely illuminated, even though the sky is streaked with
color. But as the sun emerges from the cloudy horizon,
its reflection flashing a flickering golden streak across
the ocean to the beach, suddenly the world around me
is aglow with the shimmering reflections of the iced
dune grasses and elaeagnus bushes and the sparkling icicles that adorn every tree, bench and railing. It is the
most beautiful morning I have ever seen.*

*Susan is now standing beside me, her hand on my shoul-
der. "Incredible," she says, looking at me, "incredible."*

*"Thanks, honey," I say, "I appreciate the compli-
ment, but you should have seen the sunrise."*

Chapter 14

Christmas
of **change**

Christmas brings a change in the weather and children to the beach house. The grandchildren are wonderful to have around, and Jack and I truly enjoy their company. But extended visits with them now, as a group, reaffirm what I've known for some time: My energy and stamina are waning. I remember my mother saying when my children were young, "My get up and go has got up and went." She was an English teacher who would occasionally use bad grammar to emphasize a point.

Preparing for Christmas, I am content to do very little decorating, using the excuse that it is someone else's house and I'm not going to drag in a tree and a lot of pine branches that I'll have to sweep up later.

Jack goes along with it, but a Christmas tree is very special to him. Deep-rooted traditions, involving treasured childhood experiences, are difficult to abandon. So Jack puts up what he describes as a "Christmas dune decoration" that Angel watches him decorate and I photograph.

The idea begins when I spot some kind of tumbleweed being rolled up the beach by the wind. It is tan rather than green and less than two feet high, but its branches curve up gracefully. I stick it in the sand of the cove in front of our porch, and decorate it with sea debris washed up on the beach. I drape it with strings of parchment-like capsules, which are the egg

Christmas Of Change

cases of a mollusk called a whelk. Red and green sea-weed add color, and various spiral-shaped shells from whelk, snails and gastropods serve as ornaments. My father would have laughed, as Susan does, but he would have approved, as she does.

This is the first year I have not decorated a pine tree with multicolored lights, ornaments and tinsel, the way my father had. Among his accomplishments, Pop was an artist. Although his formal schooling ended with the sixth grade, he later studied at the Maryland Institute of Art and, for him, a Christmas tree was a work of art — the lights strung first in a balanced pattern, then the glass balls and figurines arranged symmetrically and, along with the carefully draped tinsel, aligned with the lights to catch and reflect their glowing hues. He always let me help select and decorate the tree, and that is among my favorite memories. Trimming the tree took hours. My mother fussed with Pop, but he blissfully ignored her.

Christmas tree decorating at our home is the same as that of my childhood in West Baltimore. Susan fusses at my fussing with the tree for hours, but she does it affec-tionately, aware of how close I feel to my father while trying to do it exactly as he did. And when my son was growing up, he also helped me select and trim the tree, as I had done with my father, which made me feel even closer to Pop, because then I began to understand how he must have felt about me.

When my sister and I grew up and left home, my father finally let go of the tree tradition, gave in to my mother and bought a fake tree. However, he could never fake his dislike for it. And now that our children are grown and most of our grandchildren are teen-agers, it's probably time for me to let go of that tradition too. But hey, Pop, as Bogie might have said, we'll always have West Baltimore.

I don't think Jack's traditional tree is gone forever. I have a collec-tion of angel ornaments that I love getting out and hanging on the tree. O'Donnell gives me a new one each Christmas (they come with granddaughter Emily's name on the gift tag). I'd be so disappointed if that stopped, or if I had no reason to get the others out to put on display. And if Christopher has a child, I'm sure Jack will quickly resume the live Christmas tree ritual. So the traditions will be resurrected periodically, to be savored, discussed and passed on.

But I love our dune tree — no fuss, no muss. I also hung a wreath of white lights that I brought from home. Last year, it was on our barn, so you could see it driving up to our house. I also reasoned that the perfect place for a Christmas wreath was on a stable. This year, I put it on the front of the beach house, under the trellis that holds the wisteria vine. In the laundry room, tucked away on a shelf, I found two strands of decorative lights. "Perfect," I said aloud, feeling a surge of youthful energy. The lights, I suspected, were used by the owners as festive decorations for summer parties. But, to me, they seemed perfect for Christmas at the beach. Two colorful strands of illuminated parrots and palm trees — green palm trees and red and yellow parrots. Parrots and palm trees for Christmas in Dewey Beach, near the parrots of Silver Lake. I wrapped them around the railing on the walk over the dunes, so that not only could we see them from the house, but people walking the beach at night could enjoy them as well.

My favorite spot of Christmas color is a beautiful red amaryllis, given to us by JoAnn Rogers, a friend of the people who own the beach house we're renting. We met JoAnn when she came to the house with her 2-year-old daughter, Maddie, to take pictures of Maddie on the beach for their Christmas card. JoAnn promised at that time that we'd meet her husband, Paul, after Christmas, when he'd bring their tree to deposit between the snow fence and the dunes. She says it's one of their traditions, that helps shore up the protective barrier.

On Christmas morning, buoyed by the beauty of the day and eagerly awaiting the arrival of my daughter, Marjorie, and her boys, Jay and Tommy, I go out into the winter wonderland to get the papers and am greeted with a surprise. There, on the front page of the *Delaware State News*, is a picture of me, walking in the snow on the Rehoboth Beach boardwalk. On Christmas Eve, as I was walking into town, I looked up through the falling snow to see a woman with a camera pointed my way. She asked if she could take my picture. I

Christmas Of Change

laughed and said, "You don't want a picture of me like this." Dressed in my bulky coat and boots, with my hat pulled down over my eyes, I was sure I looked like some homeless person. "I've already taken it," she said, "I'm with the *Delaware State News*. Would you mind giving me your name, in case we use it?"

"Sure, why not?" I said, feeling certain they wouldn't use it. Knowing how news organizations work and what makes a good headline or front-page picture, I was sure they'd find a scene such as Jack saw — the child sledding on the sand dune. But there I am, and I do look like a vagrant. "Wait until I show Jack." The thought makes me chuckle, "Won't he be proud?"

Christmas with my daughter and the boys goes well. She is also happy about the change in scene and tradition. This is the second Christmas of her separation from her husband,and last year, at home, had been hard. I give gifts bought at the beach stores, souvenirs to remind her of this holiday at the shore. One gift, new flannel sheets, I put on the four-poster bed Marjorie's sleeping in, and I tell her to take the sheets with her when she leaves — a nice gift for her, I think, and less laundry for me. The boys get name-brand clothes from the Rehoboth Outlets, as they'd requested. In fact, I spend the next two days driving them back and forth to the outlets so they can spend the other Christmas money they've brought with them. It seems that teen and pre-teen boys are just as fashion-conscious these days, and like to shop just as much, as girls.

After a dinner of prime roast beef and "chocolate lust" from Rita's Desserts, I insist that we all pile into the car to go look at the Christmas lights. The Rehoboth Beach lights elicit sounds of gleeful appreciation — the town decorations, Mayor Cooper's tree and the floating trees of Silver Lake. But then I push the patience of the adolescent boys by urging Jack to drive down the coast to see the lights of Ocean City. Before we reach Bethany, the young voices from the back seat begin asking, "Where are we going?" They haven't seen any notable display of Christmas lights for at least 10 minutes. "We're going to Ocean City to see what I'm told are spectacular lights down there," I say. "Oh no!" they groan in unison. "Where in Ocean City?" they ask. "Well," I respond cheerfully, "maybe all the way down to the inlet," not sure where the main display is. "To the inlet?" My daughter's voice has joined the chorus. We stop at a con-

Christmas Of Change

venience store for ice cream and pound cake to pacify the boys and perhaps keep them quiet on the drive down the coast. Tommy, who didn't want any "chocolate lust," eats half the pound cake.

Sorry, Rita, he's 11 years old; his taste will mature.

Not far across the Maryland line, in north Ocean City, we see the lights. "There," I say, "look. There it is — there's the Festival of Lights." A cheer erupts from everyone, including Jack.

First it is just Tommy and I who want to ride the train through the extensive exhibit of action figures, outlined with colored lights. Then everyone agrees. "We're here," Jack says, "it's only a dollar a person, let's do it." Excitedly and feeling the urge to be close, especially for me without coat or gloves, we huddle together, oohing and ahhing, as we ride through the large amusement-park size compound of animated lights.

On the way back to Rehoboth Beach, Marjorie and the boys alternate between singing Christmas carols and Boy Scout camp songs. Tommy eats the rest of the pound cake. And although this is an experience we will probably never repeat, I sense it is one the boys will remember and most likely tell their children about. Even if we haven't established a new tradition, we've created a warm memory, in this our season of change.

Chapter 15

Boys' Adventure

On the Monday after Christmas, Marjorie goes home, but her sons, Jay and Tommy, stay with us. They will soon be joined by our three other grandsons, Brian, David and Alex, whose father, Steve, is driving them part of the way here. I've agreed to meet them in Denton, Md., so Steve doesn't have to make the entire roundtrip to the beach. I drive up after dinner, and it is dark when the boys pile into my car, and we head back.

All five boys had pleaded to visit us together at the beach during the Christmas vacation. Five boys — three almost 14, one 11 and one 10 — in a beach house, in December, with their grandparents and no computer games. In planning their visit, I had reasoned that, even if the weather turned cold, they would still be able to enjoy playing football on the beach or playing ball with Angel. And I was planning several bicycle trips, which also gave me an idea for their Christmas gifts. Three of the boys needed new bikes, so I suggested to Jack that we go back to our new friend, Frank, at Atlantic Cycles, for three more great deals, which is what we did. Three boys' mountain bikes for $30 each or $85 for the three. That included new front tires on two of them.

The first morning, the boys race around town — around Silver Lake, to the convenience store, then up on the boardwalk, sliding with glee on the remaining ice. They ride to the shops, finding many of interest. At Imagination, Tommy finds a magnetic earring. They all

Boys' Adventure

love Chesapeake Kites and Flags. They discover, over and over again, that the beach town of Rehoboth does not shut down at Christmas time and that it is child-friendly and safe. They ride nonstop all morning. Their first day with us is going as planned. However, in the early afternoon it begins to rain, and continues raining for the next three days.

Fortunately, the beach house is equipped with a VCR. We rent six movies in two days. We buy 3-D puzzles and shop at the outlets. Even so, I think the two things most responsible for keeping their visit from ending with frayed nerves and bad moods are a toy and a talk.

First, yo-yos are popular again. And they are a great release for pent-up adolescent energies. The secret for adults in a beach house with five yo-yos going at once is to make rules about where they can be spun, swung, walked and rocked, and these adults need to sit still, with appropriate appreciation, for yo-yo shows.

The hero, however, in this activity is Randy, the "Yo-Yo Man " at Chesapeake Kites and Flags, on Rehoboth Avenue. The boys ride through the rain to spend time with Randy and listen to him talk about the weight and balance and abilities of various yo-yos. He watches tricks and gives pointers. And if it gets a little loud in the beach house,

I say, "Go see Randy. Show him that new trick," and off they go. Randy has the patience of a saint, or maybe it's just the off-season luxury of time, without crowds, that gives everyone here such good dispositions.

The other thing, the talk, I delivered to the boys the first night. I had spoken with Jay and Tommy before going to pick up the other boys. And then I talked to Brian, David and Alex on the way down in the car. These boys are good kids, but good or not, five boys can be, shall we say, overzealous and impatient with one another, whether they're related or not. Actually, being related seems to make it easier to get into spats. On other family vacations when we were all together, there had been a couple of unpleasant incidents, when one or two of the boys were being picked on or shut out of something. Often, such situations erupt into fights, hard feelings, tears and reprimands. I wanted none of that this time.

I told the boys many things in my talk, such as, "This vacation was your idea, so make the most of it by being cooperative." But I think the most significant comment I made had to do with my feelings. Reflecting on my words and their reactions, I think this one statement made the biggest impression on them. I had never said anything like it before.

What I said was, "You're all my grandchildren, and I love you all very much. When you argue or don't get along, it's extremely upsetting for me. I don't want to be upset or have reason to be unhappy during this visit."

Boys are just as sensitive as girls; actually, I think more so, but unfortunately we, as a society, teach them to hide it. I'm convinced that my grandsons were so concerned about my feelings and not wanting to upset me that it affected their behavior.

They have been wonderful the whole stay — pleasant and polite and helpful to one another. Even the two cousins, who have been known to roll around on the floor, faces red with anger, literally at each other's throats, spend time together building a puzzle and showing each other yo-yo tricks. And the older boys, who often spend enormous energy trying to get away from the younger ones, include them in everything.

At the end of the stay, with tears, I tell them how proud I am of them and what a wonderful time I've had, thanks to them. Their only regret and mine is that we didn't have those bicycle trips.

Chapter 16

New**Year**

Our friends, Andy and Toba Barth, greet us with hugs and the exclamation, "You look great!" which, at our age, usually means, "I thought you'd look worse." But they mean it, and we feel it. It is New Year's Eve, which means dinner with the Barths, the one holiday tradition we are able to maintain at the beach. We've been celebrating New Year's Eve with them ever since Andy, Susan and I worked together at WMAR-TV in Baltimore. Our annual ritual involves good conversation, assorted wines, big lobsters, thick steaks and decadent chocolate desserts. Another mutual friend of ours once asked if it wouldn't be simpler to just use an IV and inject cholesterol directly into our veins.

Although Andy is more than a decade younger than I am, we share many interests. But food is near the top of the list for both of us, especially the kind that the food police say is bad. But Andy and I also exercise a lot: running, lifting weights, playing tennis. We both know that the more we exercise, the more we can eat. Actually, most of our meals consist of the recommended stuff: fish, chicken, vegetables, fruit and grains, but we occasionally "reward" ourselves by eating really good "bad" stuff.

Andy is still quite lean. Me, well, my son says I'm stocky; I like that. But my mirror says something else. Although I exercise every day and weigh only three or four pounds more than in my lean, hard youth, nature (i.e. gravity and the loss of skin elasticity) has rearranged everything.

My face has been slowly falling into my neck for some time now. My son, when he was a young boy, enjoyed grabbing and jiggling the already flabby folds around my jaw line, until I made a rule that he could play with anything in the house except my face. There's been a similar fleshy slide from my chest to my waist, and the skin covering my elbows and knees now sags. My body would probably be even baggier and saggier if the muscle underneath had not been maintained. Because of weightlifting, I really haven't lost any muscle or strength. The "use it or lose it" theory is also supported by extensive scientific research. According to virtually every study I've read, exercise may be the closest thing there is to a fountain of youth. Elderly people who have been bedridden or confined to wheelchairs have walked again after trying a weightlifting program. Recent studies also indicate that aerobic exercises, such as walking, running, biking and swimming, are not only good for the heart and lungs, but also stimulate the brain and improve memory. That's why many people refuse to take aging sitting down.

Let me quickly add, at the insistence of our attorneys, that no one should begin any exercise program without first consulting a doctor. Aging well is also an attitude. The acclaimed architect, Frank Lloyd Wright, who created his greatest works after he turned 65, said, "To me, aging has no meaning. Youth is a quality, a quality that is ageless."

And Satchel Paige, who continued pitching in the major leagues until he was apparently in his 50s — no one is really sure — was always being asked about his seeming agelessness. "How old would you be," he once replied, "if you didn't know how old you was?"

Life expectancy at the turn of the 20th century was 47; at the start of the new millennium, it is 76. According to data presented at the Global Meeting of Generations, within the next 50 years, there will be more people over 60 than those under the age of 15, which is unprecedented. And the fastest-growing population segment is that of people who are more than 80 years old. Researchers say that if you make it to 65, you can expect to live another 25 years. So prepare for the future. You have one, probably a long one. Passing 50 just means you've started the second 50, that is, if the shock of receiving that AARP membership notice doesn't kill you.

The fear of aging is called gerontophobia. Many people fear aging, because to them it defines loss — the loss of hair, looks, health, hearing, sight and memory. So, who wants to go there? I didn't. But fortunately, I've lived long enough to get there and to find what my older friends have been telling me is true. It can be the best time of our lives. And there are now remedies that can limit most of those "losses," including medicines for memory loss, although I can't remember what they are. Psychologist Paul Costa says one National Institute on Aging study, monitoring the minds of the aging, shows that worries about memory loss are unfounded. "The busy 50-year-old executive forgets where he misplaced something, and is now in a panic, thinking, 'Is this an early sign of Alzheimer's disease?' But 10-15 years earlier, when he misplaced things, he wasn't as concerned about it, even though it happened with the same frequency."

The perception that we get grumpier as we get older is also a misconception. One NIA study found that personality does not change with age; grumpy old men were also grumpy young men.

New Year

What makes some people grumpy is worrying about their age. Don't dwell on the fact that if you're in your 60s, as I am, you're now older than most of the people in the world. Incidentally, if you weren't aware of the fact until now, please accept my apology and put it out of your mind. Also, remember that exercise can make you feel younger, which may improve your disposition.

For me, one of the most important lessons about staying physically fit was taught to me by my son, Christopher, when he was still a baby. One day, soon after he was born, I was giving him a bath. As I rubbed his stomach, I discovered rock hard abdominal muscles — abs — beneath the soft plump surface. It felt like a washboard under there, as I probed gently with my fingers. That day I began what is still a daily routine of sit-ups and leg raises, because I reasoned that if nature deems it necessary for us to be born with such firm abdominal muscles, it's probably a good idea to keep them that way. So now my stomach is like a newborn's — rock hard, under a soft, pudgy surface.

Chapter 17

Best
Friends

Fog hovers over the wet sand. The sun, trying to burn through, is only a hazy circle in the afternoon sky. We have just returned to the beach after a week at home, a week that involved a severe ice storm, with downed trees, power outages and many accidents in the Baltimore/Washington area. Here, the mild, damp weather is a relief, and the forecast says the dampness will soon be gone.

We're elated to be back. Even Angel bounces excitedly, so happy she seems to smile. Jack takes her with him on a walk up the beach. They disappear into the fog, walking an hour or more into the now familiar territory that stretches beyond the Rehoboth Beach boardwalk.

The routine of walking and exercising Angel, on the beach and in the ocean, has been one of the most pleasant parts of our time at the shore. And from what we've observed, it is "quality time" for all the dogs and their owners who live here full-time or those just visiting. I find myself wondering if people relocate here because they have dogs, or if they get dogs after they come, realizing what a nice place it is for them.

Dogs are welcome at the beach, but there are rules and regulations concerning them. In Dewey Beach, along with many other public beaches along the Maryland/Delaware shore, from Memorial Day weekend through Labor Day, there are restricted beach hours for dogs. During that period, dogs are not allowed on the beach between the hours of 9:30 a.m. and 5:30 p.m.

Best Friends

Off-season, dogs are welcome anytime, but they must be controlled and you must clean up after them — rules that apply year-round. In Dewey Beach, at every street entrance to the beach are attractive white wooden street signs on which are green boxes marked "Doggy Bags." In the summer, those boxes contain white plastic bags to make it easier and convenient for dog owners to comply with the "Pooper Scooper" law. There is a $100 fine for littering, by man or man's best friend.

Off-season, people with dogs must supply their own "Doggy Bags." We save plastic grocery bags; we keep them stored in a container by the porch door and grab one each time we take Angel out on the beach. Most people have gotten into the habit of doing this, and it's a common sight to see people walking the beach with their dogs, swinging little bags of retrieved droppings. It's the dog owners without the little plastic bags who get the disapproving stares.

Having a dog on the beach can be a very social outing, for owners and dogs. But it's the canines that attract all the attention. The dogs sniff each other and then briefly play together. The owners also greet each other, but rarely exchange names, except those of their dogs. It's the shared appreciation of the dogs that stimulates conversation. Angel and I are friendly (Angel a little more so than I) with dogs named Dolly, Daisy and BooBoo. There's a little dog named Lucy, a St. Bernard named Sophie, and a golden retriever named Birdie. There's Rocky and George and Bethany.

Just the other day, we met a playful 8-month-old Chesapeake Bay retriever named "Bos'n" or "Boatswain," depending on your preference. "A Bos'n," the dog's owner explained, "is a ship's warrant officer or petty officer who's in charge of the deck crew." He went on to say that his dog Bos'n sails with him on his boat and, as if in command, "sits right up on the bow. He loves it." I could picture this beautiful dog in front of the boat, nose into the wind, ears flapping, looking like a figurehead, or perhaps one of the lovers in the movie "Titanic."

Angel and I both have picked up a few tricks out on the beach. It's amazing what animals, as well as people, can learn from watching others.

Angel sees a golden retriever digging a hole in the sand, and you can almost see the observation translate into imitation. She begins digging around her tennis ball, and when the hole gets so deep that the front part of her body is out of view and she has a hard time finding the ball, she moves it out of that hole and starts digging another one. She also moves

around the hole she is digging, widening and lengthening the crevasse. If another dog comes along the beach while she's digging she crouches down into the trench, and when the dog gets close, she jumps up to surprise the other animal. One man walking the beach stops to comment on one of Angel's more extensive crater compounds. "If that dog starts using a paper cup to mold sand castle towers, I'm calling the David Letterman show." Jack, who tries to refill all the holes so that no one falls into one of them, notes that such pet tricks are referred to as "stupid" on the Letterman show. "Clearly," I insist, "the man was implying that our dog is intelligent, not stupid."

The owner of the golden retriever named Tipper, who taught Angel to dig, inadvertently taught me a trick as well — how to eliminate the muscle strain resulting from repeatedly throwing a tennis ball out over the breakers for Angel to retrieve. I was developing considerable pain in my shoulder, neck and arm. One morning, I saw the man carrying a tennis racquet as he walked his dog, and, as I wondered why, he pulled a tennis ball out of his coat pocket, threw it up, lifted the racquet and hit the ball a good distance down the beach. The dog raced after it. "Yes," I yelled out loud, "that's it!" On our next visit home, Jack retrieved an old racquet from the back of a closet, and my arm has been fine ever since. And Angel is getting more exercise than ever. I can now hit the tennis ball out over the breakers; she jumps the waves and rides them back in.

The man with the racquet is named Mark Brown, and he explained that he had suffered a similar shoulder problem. Mark and his partner, Joe Kramer, own and operate an inn, overlooking Silver Lake, called Silver Lake. And, because many of their guests are also pet owners, they have built two apartments, separate from the others, in which they allow dogs. Later, he and Joe give us a tour of their place, and we immediately decide that this is where we'll stay with Angel when we come to the beach in-season. Jack, Angel and I now share beach banter with Mark and Tipper almost every morning and evening, as we hit our tennis balls for our dogs.

However, in Mark's case, his cure for shoulder problems, the tennis racquet, has one bad side effect — tennis elbow. He laughs as he tells us this, and he is now learning to hit with the other hand.

Best Friends

Thank goodness I haven't experienced any such problem. My arm and my "serve" are getting stronger each day, providing new experiences for Angel.

One calm day, there is a pair of ducks out beyond the gentle waves, diving for fish. The tennis ball I hit for Angel lands near them, but does not scare them away. As Angel reaches the ball, she pauses, looking from it over at the ducks, back and forth several times. Angel has never been trained to hunt, so she's never retrieved ducks, but I can see her thinking, "Something tells me I should be going after those ducks, instead of this tennis ball." She brings back the tennis ball.

Dogs and their owners are intriguing to watch, especially at the beach. It's a study in relationships — the bonding of characteristics that form a union, which is enjoyable for both animal and human. It's been said that a dog often takes on the appearance and mannerisms of the owner, or is it the other way around? I describe Angel and me as "big boned blondes." Jack calls us his girls, or if he's upset with us, that word for female dogs.

There's a man and dog duo that passes our beach house each morning and afternoon. Jack has dubbed them "The Red Ball Express," not because they are fast, but because they are so slow and because a red ball is all that keeps them moving.

In silhouette against the ocean, the man, who has a large stomach, resembles the late Alfred Hitchcock. Each day, he lumbers along the beach, erect, never bending, walking his elderly black and white sheep dog, which mostly stands and sniffs. To make the dog move, the Hitchcockian figure repeatedly kicks a small red ball along the sand, not very hard and not very far. The dog doesn't so much chase it as stroll after it, at almost the same pace as its master, then stops and sniffs some more. Most of the time, the dog does not pick up the ball. If he does, he advances it a short way. He never brings it back to the man, but waits for the man to come to the ball. The man never bends to pick up the ball and throw it; he just kicks it as he continues shuffling along in a straight line, almost like a target in a shooting gallery, because after traveling a

Best Friends

short distance he turns and repeats the same slow, methodical process — kick, walk, dog sniffs, kick, walk, dog sniffs — back to where the man and dog entered the beach. Only then does the man finally bend over, as if taking a bow, but it is only to retrieve the little red ball, which seems to propel both man and beast along the beach.

Companionship and commitment propel most of us along the beach with our dogs, seeing to their needs, and in exchange they give us unconditional love and regular exercise; although, as Jack has noted, some get more than others. Many people run with their dogs, Jack among them. And for him, as with many joggers, the time spent running often helps shape thoughts, as well as the body.

This off-season time at the beach, with Angel by his side, has given Jack the opportunity to think about what he's done right with his life, what he's done wrong and what he holds dear. I doubt if anyone has reached the age of retirement and not gone through this self-analysis. I think it's a very beneficial exercise, especially if, like Jack, you share it with those who people your thoughts.

Dec. 7, Warm, balmy, Bermuda-like weather. Running along the beach, wearing nothing but a bathing suit, I say to our dog, "Can you believe it's December 7th?" As usual, Angel stubbornly refuses to reply. Or maybe she didn't hear me, because I said it so softly, afraid that Mother Nature might overhear and realize that she'd forgotten to change the weather when we changed our calenders.

I've never been able to persuade Susan to run, jog or do any kind of regular exercise. To her, it's boring and a waste of energy. She stays in shape by using that energy to cut the grass, dig fence post holes, plant flowers and trees and other such productive endeavors. Good help is not hard to find if you marry it. Susan laughs when I say things like that. Other women don't. Other women and most men, occasion-

*ally even my son, wonder why she loves me and con-
tinues to live with me. So do I. However, I just accept
it because, like a perfect golf swing, if you analyze it
too much, you might lose it. I've never had a perfect
golf swing, but my wife and marriage are as close to
perfect as I can imagine and losing her would be
unimaginably painful.*

*My son's love for me may be a little more understand-
able. I was, I think, a good father. Look, it's easy for me
to be modest about most of my so-called accomplishments — but being a father, despite my share of mistakes, was by far the best thing I ever did. Even his
mother, my ex-wife, says, "Jack was a good father —
lousy husband — but a good father."*

*My son is now in his late 20s, and we are close
friends, in addition to the father-son relationship. The
principled way he lives his life, both personally and
professionally, makes me extremely proud.*

Standing on the dune steps, I watch Jack coming down the beach;
Angel is leading the way. She pauses, looks back and waits. "Good
girl! Good stay!" he praises. They both look tired, but content. When
she sees me, Angel runs ahead. Jack smiles as he approaches, leans
down to pet the dog, rubbing her head with affectionate vigor. "She
was good," he says, looking up at me. "A good girl."

It seems to me that if you can include the word friend in the
description of any relationship, it's sure to be a good one, and that
includes the tie humans have with their dogs. Because, for many of
us, they fit our definition of a friend — devoted, sharing unconditional love and unquestioned loyalty. There's an element of ease in
the company of a true friend, who demands little, but gives much.

Chapter 18

The
Cape

The Cape

Cape Henlopen State Park, with giant sand dunes overlooking the Atlantic Ocean, is where the coastal shoreline curves around into the Delaware Bay. There are miles of beaches on this cape, where swimming and fishing are allowed. The park, with 3,785 acres open to the public, includes pine forests, saltwater marsh lands, fresh water wetlands and Gordons Pond, which is a man-made coastal impoundment. (Access to this pond is from the southern entrance to the state park, which is at the northern end of Rehoboth Beach. The main entrance to the park is 1 mile east of Lewes, just a half-mile beyond the Cape May/Lewes Ferry Terminal.)

Off-season, the good news is that there is no charge to enter Cape Henlopen State Park. The bad news is that some areas might be closed or only open on weekends.

Standing at the point of the cape, you can watch the gleaming white ferry boats glide in and out of the terminal through the Harbor of Refuge, so named because of the historic breakwaters that created a safe shelter for ships fleeing storms. The picturesque lighthouses that mark the east end of each of the two breakwaters attract artists and photographers, both from land and those passing at sea. Area art shows almost always include several artistic or photographic renderings of these familiar beacons.

Jack and I have visited Cape Henlopen several times, concentrating on specific areas each visit. On a warm winter day in late January, we walk the beach to see the great dunes from the ocean side. We park in space provided at the head of the Dune Overlook Trail, but walk the other way, across a surf fishing road to the beach.

The road is actually a deep, sandy path strewn with an odd assortment of rocks, some mineralized, others that appear to be volcanic and so much coal that a long stretch of the sand is almost black. (Later at the Nature Center, we are told that the rocks are apparently the discarded ballast of old cargo ships. The coal was either washed ashore from shipwrecks or a remnant of coal shipments that were once brought ashore at this location. Another possibility is that it came from trains when there was a railroad on the cape to supply its military base.)

As we enter the ocean side of Cape Henlopen, we see the Great Dune, described in the brochures as the highest sand dune between Cape Hatteras and Cape Cod. We overhear other people express the same disappointment we feel. The dune is pretty, but seems meager compared to the dunes at Provincetown.

However, there are other truly rare delights here. Around many of the clumps of dune grass, we see mysterious circles in the sand. Some of the softly etched designs are only an inch wide, but others are much larger. Some are complete circles, others just semicircles. They are the only markings in the otherwise undisturbed sand — no trails leading to or away from them. The solution to this mystery arrives with a puff of wind, which gently bends and moves the tip of the dune grass along one arc of the circle, and as the wind shifts, the grass is moved in a different direction to draw another section of the circle.

Along the shoreline are remnants of an old cedar forest. Jagged stumps of the still beautiful wood jut out of the sand at odd angles, dark brown at their base; the tops are a smooth gleaming tan, buffeted and polished by wind, sand and sea. This once tall

The Cape

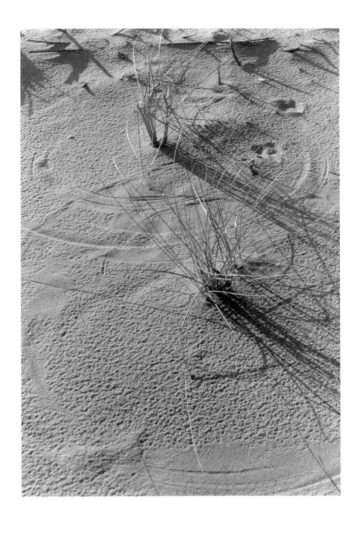

cedar forest, now buried under sand, is a dramatic reminder that these dunes and beaches, which seem so permanent, are constantly moving and changing shape and can bury buildings that man creates, as well as nature's creations.

In addition to the miles of beaches and sandy paths throughout the park, there are three miles of paved trails that can be used for bicycling and in-line skating, as well as for walking. These paths, along with the roadways, connect the main sightseeings attractions of the cape: the dune overlook, the seaside nature center, the bathhouse/ swimming area and the only World War II observation tower that's open to the public.

Off-season, the 70-foot observation tower is open only on weekends in good weather. On one bright February day, Jack and I, with weekend guests, find the tower door unlocked and swung wide. Delighted, we enter the circular, concrete structure to climb the winding, black, metal staircase — 113 steps — to the open platform on top. The cadence of our footsteps reverberate within the narrow walls, in which viewing slots had

The Cape

been cut, so that soldiers could scan the ocean for enemy submarines. From these slots, shafts of golden sunlight pierce the darkness at various levels of our climb. We stop to peer out at each opportunity.

With us are friends we met in Bermuda, and with whom we reunite each September, when we go back for our annual visit. One couple, from Philadelphia, is younger — mid-50s and not yet retired. The other couple from New Jersey, is older. She's 79, he's 80 and has been retired for almost 20 years. This couple, Marjorie and Charlie Raynor, though older, are often the ones to suggest the more energetic undertakings. Charlie is the first to reach the top of the tower and the last to descend. He and Jack agree that the soldiers who had this duty may have been bored, but it was safe and their view was terrific.

Spread out before us are miles of ocean and the Delaware Bay, giving a clear picture of the conflicting currents sweeping around the point of the cape. To the south, nestled into the great dunes, are old bunkers and a crumbling, vine-covered, abandoned World War II Army fort. In 1941, the Army turned 543 acres of the cape into a military base, Fort Miles, as part of the Atlantic coastal defense against any possible German invasion. Cannons were embedded in the dunes to shoot at any German subs that might be spotted by the sentinels in the observation towers. At the end of the war, one German sub surrendered here. The German crew that came ashore was imprisoned for a time in the Fort Miles stockade.

In 1964, the Department of Defense declared Fort Miles surplus property and turned it over to the State of Delaware to become part of the Cape Henlopen State Park.

Looking beyond the dunes, you can see two more towers out on the beach. On this day, the ocean, at high tide, is washing around them, with waves splashing against the weathered, rust-stained sides of these citadels that have stood this seemingly vulnerable ground for more than half a century.

To the west of the beach towers is Gordons Pond, a large body of brackish water, called a coastal impoundment. It was created out of a natural depression, just west of the shoreline, that was used in the 1800s for a saltworks operation. By drawing off and boiling away the ocean water that flooded the area during high tides, salt was collected.

Gordons Pond was established by bulldozing dikes on the ocean side of the area and then filling it with water pumped in from the

Lewes/Rehoboth canal on the opposite side. This coastal impoundment is co-managed by the Delaware Parks Department and the Fish
and Wildlife Agency of the Department of Natural Resources.

The pond is a habitat for wildlife, but is also used to help control the
Lewes/Rehoboth Beach mosquito population. One way this is done is
by stocking the pond with a little minnow-sized fish named Killi-fish
that eat mosquito larvae. One fish can eat up to 2500 larvae a day.

Another way is by raising and lowering the levels of the pond
water. Keeping the water high during mating season is a form of birth
control, because most mosquitoes like swampy areas with low or no
water to breed in. There are 55 species of mosquitoes in Delaware,
and some do lay eggs on the surface of high water, but the Killi-fish
get the larvae of those mosquitoes. In the spring, Gordons Pond is
lowered to give the pond's plants, which the wintering waterfowl
have eaten back, a chance to grow.

Unlike the salt marshes of Indian River State Park, with small
streams and rivulets of water running through muddy, grass-choked
marsh land, this pond encompasses 350 acres. An expansive body of
still water, its calm surface is a mirror reflection of tall grasses, pine
trees and drift wood along the banks. The entire area known as
Gordons Pond takes up more than 1,000 acres, which is naturally and
unnaturally preserved. Winter is a good time to visit the pond, when
there are no mosquitoes around to disturb its serene, pristine beauty.

Looking farther south from the top of the observation tower, you
can see the taller buildings on the boardwalk of Rehoboth Beach.
Turning to the west, you view the roof tops and church steeples of the
town of Lewes.

After the trek back down the tower steps, our friend Marjorie says,
"Well, I guess that was our stress test for this year — and we passed."
Marjorie is a petite woman (she had to use a stool to climb up into the
four-poster bed at the beach house) who has kept her shape with exercise
and a careful diet. She had a hip replacement several years ago, but says
there has been no pain or discomfort, so she can still take long walks
almost every day and live a very active life. Her interest in books and
movies and staying involved and trying new things has not abated with
age. My father would have said, "Marjorie Raynor has a lot of 'pep.'"

It was Marjorie who suggested, one night in Bermuda, that we have
a beach party and go for a midnight swim. We did, carrying a bottle

The Cape

of white wine and glasses out to a raft — and enjoyed the most fun of that year's trip. Charlie is the same way, refusing to act or be labeled old. He walks the beach with energy, at a rapid pace, quick-stepping as he plays with our dog, kicking her tennis ball like a soccer ball. At home, he has a boat and loves being out on the water; he volunteers at the hospital library, entering medical information into the computer system, and he plays golf several times a week. The Raynors stay physically and mentally active. Our younger friends from Philadelphia, Joyce and Frank Gildea, call them their heroes, and say they want to be just like them when they "grow up."

Out on Cape Henlopen's point, the Raynors are not content to simply read the signs about the migratory birds and horseshoe crab connection. They walk down to inspect the beach where that connection occurs each spring.

> The horseshoe crab, which has survived since the time of dinosaurs, is not really a crab, but a marine arachnid, which means that it's a relative of spiders and scorpions. Under its shell, which looks like Darth Vader's helmet, the crab has 10 hairy legs, like a huge tarantula and, like the scorpion, it has a tail, all of which make it appear fearsome. However, it's harmless.
>
> They're seen on beaches all along the East Coast, but the largest population is in the Delmarva area, and their favorite honeymoon spots are on the beaches of Delaware Bay. Considering the horseshoe crab's appearance, you may wonder how they make love. They fantasize about the more delicate and shapely blue crab. Of course, that's just a theory.
>
> What we do know is that, every spring, the horseshoe crabs come ashore with the high tide for their nocturnal mating ritual, each female carrying one or more males on her back. (Susan claims that females of every species have a similar burden.) They drag the males along the sand to fertilize the thousands of eggs deposited there by each female. The only sound of their mating is the gentle clacking of their shells. The night we watched, a mist hung over the area. Or

The Cape

was that cigarette smoke?

While mating, many of the horseshoe crabs are flipped over. The next morning, they are lying on their backs, claws churning, their spike-like tails probing the sand, trying to right themselves. Some will be saved by the rising tide, but others will bake in the sun, vulnerable to predators.

The fertilized eggs will hatch in two weeks, each a fraction of an inch in size. But most will never reach that stage, because migrating shorebirds, hundreds of thousands of them, tired and hungry after their non-stop flight from South America, where they winter, have learned to time their flight for a layover at Delaware Bay, so that they can feed on the horseshoe crabs' eggs. The beaches pulsate with the massive feeding frenzy of sanderlings, sandpipers, red knots, plovers, willets — at least 20 species in all. The air is filled with their clamorous cries. The sight and sound attract many tourists.

Revitalized by the food and rest, the birds eventually resume the arduous journey to their own breeding grounds, in the Arctic. Experts say that these birds would probably not survive without this feeding ground.

The horseshoe crabs may also be endangered, not by the birds — enough of their eggs have always survived the birds to ensure the crabs' survival — but because horseshoe crabs, once used for fertilizer, are now being extensively harvested for bait, a major source of income for watermen, who have been hurt by a dwindling supply of oysters. Delaware, Maryland and New Jersey have imposed restrictions to limit the crab harvests.

Their blood is also used in medical research and to detect bacteria in drug testing. But, after horseshoe crabs are bled, they are returned to their natural habitat. To help ensure their survival, Maryland is tracking them. Anyone who finds one with a tag attached is asked to notify the Department of Natural Resources.

Whenever Susan and I see a horseshoe crab stranded upside down on the beach, we toss it back into the ocean. After each wave breaks, the crab's spikey tail sticks out of the water like a submarine's periscope, struggling for several minutes before clearing the breakers. Horseshoe crabs can live for many decades. The shells of the older ones are encrusted with barnacles, mussels and similar small creatures. Compared with that, wrinkles and gray hair don't seem so bad.

As Jack mentioned, the spectacle of beaches filled with horseshoe crabs and shorebirds has become a popular, much anticipated tourist attraction. The crabs usually come ashore in mid-May, but exactly when is determined by the phases of the moon and the tides. However, people often get upset when the park staff can't give them a specific day and time. It's the most asked question they get. One woman called the Cape Henlopen Nature Center saying she was planning to come over from Cape May for the event and wanted to know when it would happen, so she could determine which ferry to take. Exasperated, the woman at the Nature Center said, "I don't know; I think the crabs are coming in on a Greyhound bus at noon."

Chapter 19

The
Singer

In the corner of the elegant Victorian dining room of the Atlantic Hotel in Berlin, Md., a pianist and a singer rehearse several songs they'll perform the next day at another hotel, Dunes Manor in Ocean City. The words and notes of a timeless love song fill the room and spill out into the hallway, stopping hotel guests, who pause to listen to the rich voice of cabaret-style vocalist Fran Mahr.

At the piano, composer/teacher/musicologist Bill Messenger conducts the rehearsal, "Softer — not so much vibrato," he directs. Bill, educated in musical composition at the Peabody Conservatory, with two master's degrees from the Johns Hopkins University, now spends a great deal of his time teaching older, adult students, both with the Elderhostel programs and the continuing studies classes at various colleges and universities. Just before this rehearsal session, in this same room, Bill had been the featured lecturer/performer at a luncheon sponsored by the University of Maryland Eastern Shore. Many of those in attendance were older adult students; the others were retirees and residents of the Eastern Shore. The appreciative audience was treated to a presentation on the history of ragtime, a mixture of interesting facts and lively piano playing, demonstrating the music of the popular composers of that musical genre.

Now, with Fran, Bill Messenger goes over a new song he has written that he wants her to try. "This song needs a mature singer to make sense," he explains to her. She smiles, gently swings her head to the beat as she reads the notes as well as the words. Her soft gray hair, cut in a short, pixie style, dances across her forehead. She begins without accompaniment, her voice clear, the notes true, "September sighs at summer; See how the seasons fly by; Maple trees turn redder than roses; My, how the leaves fly by; Green is a golden memory..."

The sunlight, filtering through the stained glass above the cafe curtains, gradually fades as the two musicians work into late afternoon, repeating the song over and over, searching for just the right phrasing and tone.

Fran and Bill have known each other, and periodically worked together for almost 30 years. They met at Center Stage in Baltimore. Their careers have crossed often; their friendship deepens each time. Their Dunes Manor Hotel appearance will be the first time that Fran has performed with Bill at one of his Elderhostel presentations.

Jack and I have also been friends with Fran and her husband, Mac, for many years. So we invited them to stay with us in "our" off-season beach house while they were in the neighborhood. In fact, in past years, it was often at the beach, in-season, that we saw each other most, when we both had summer places in north Ocean City and then later in Fenwick Island.

Fran and Mac now spend much of the year at their home in Florida, and, unfortunately, we see them less. But this visit allowed us to catch up on things, including their experience with Elderhostel.

Elderhostel, we're discovering, is sweeping the country and the world, as well as the Delmarva Peninsula. It is a nonprofit organization that caters to the educational and adventurous needs and desires of people over 55. It was started in 1975, in New England, as a summer-only program. It now offers 10,000 programs year-round, worldwide, to more than a quarter-of-a-million people.

Elderhostel is an extensive network of educational and cultural sites. The hosts, or sponsors, who conduct the classes and arrange the lodging include colleges, universities, conference centers, state and national parks, museums, theaters, environmental/outdoor educational centers and many others. The United States catalog lists the American programs by states, the foreign ones by countries.

When Fran and Mac arrived for their stay with us, they had just returned from a business trip to the West Coast, where they also had their first Elderhostel experience. Mac, who started his second career at age 65, designing and consulting on Yellow Page advertising and writing the definitive book on the subject, had to speak at conferences in Las Vegas and San Diego. With a gap of about a week between the appearances, he booked a five-day Elderhostel program on musical theater, which he felt certain Fran would enjoy. Sponsored by San Diego State University, it was held at a hotel in the historic Old Town section of the city.

The initial reaction of many people attending their first Elderhostel and walking into a room full of elder students for the first time is, "I'm too young for this." It's human nature not to recognize ourselves as getting older. When I took my mother-in-law out to lunch at an exquisite and quite expensive restaurant in Baltimore, sitting near us around a large table were several well-dressed, beautifully coiffed, gray-haired women, who appeared to be in their 70s. My mother-in-law, who was 95, leaned over to me and said, "This looks like an old people's place."

Mac Mahr, who is 70, and Fran, who is in her mid-60s, laughed at themselves as they shared their Elderhostel "first impression" story with us. "It was like walking into a very nice assisted-living situation," said Mac. Fran continued, "I leaned over to Mac and whispered, 'We've come a long way from Club Med.'"

But, very quickly, the Mahrs found that what they had come to was an exciting place to be. It began when they chatted with the 85-year-old woman sitting next to them, who had just finished an Elderhostel in Colorado. She told them that she had vowed to do white-water rafting before her 87th birthday, and she had just done it with the program there.

Mac, an analytical man, said he made several observations about the people in the Elderhostel program they attended. "There is a thirst for knowledge by people who want to make every day count, not in a cliched way, but by really jumping into something with both feet." Even with a program such as the one they attended on musical theater, the participants weren't there just to be entertained.

"The people," Mac continued, "were education-oriented, many of them former teachers. There was no complaining about personal things — aches or pains — or family problems. Once you got into it," Mac said convincingly, "age was not a factor." And he told me that both of

The Singer

their instructors told him that they love to teach Elderhostel students, not only because they are so attentive, but also because they, the teachers, learn so much from the older, more experienced students.

Bill Messenger agrees. He says that he's gotten a great many anecdotes from his students. "I'll talk about a certain musician or composer, and a student will come up after class and tell me about meeting that person or seeing him or her perform." And Bill listened closely as Jack told of meeting one of his music idols, Erol Garner, who, despite being unable to read or write music, became a legendary jazz pianist and composer. Garner told Jack the fascinating story of how he composed "Misty."

It was during the time I worked for WBAL Radio. At a media party following one of Garner's performances in Baltimore, I approached him and offered my compliments. He was shy, which surprised me, but friendly and easy to talk with. When I told him that "Misty" was one of my all-time favorites, he smiled, and his eyes shifted away from me, as if he were looking at something only he could see. "Wanna hear how I wrote that?" he asked. He then described how, while flying home on a commercial jetliner, the music came to him as he gazed through the window at the beautiful cloud formations. He began thumping his fingers on his legs, fingering the notes he heard in his head, as if he were playing a piano, memorizing them, so that later he could play the melody on a real piano and a collaborator could transcribe the notes onto paper.

"And I was grunting," Garner continued, "You know I always grunt when I play. So here I am, pounding my fingers on my knees and grunting, and there was this lady sitting next to me, and she was looking at me as if I'd lost my mind. Finally, she said, 'What in God's name are you doing?' I kind of apologized, and I told her I was writing a song. She just looked at me and shook her head." Garner laughed at the memory, and said, "I think that convinced her I was crazy."

It's that sort of personal story that Bill Messenger loves to hear, tucking it away and pulling it out when it pertains to a class he's teaching. He has hundreds of such stories, all fascinating.

The Concert: It's 10 a.m. and we're at the Dunes Manor Hotel, overlooking the ocean. A strong March wind bends the tall grasses into the snow fencing lining the path across the dunes. The gusts engage the single line of empty rocking chairs that stretch across the large oceanfront porch. It seems as if the chairs are being moved by the memory of former guests.

In a conference room, just off the porch, 25 people sit at rows of tables, which hold pads of paper and pencils, pitchers of water and glasses. In front of the room: a TV monitor with a VCR, a large movie screen and an electric piano.

Bill Messenger is talking about "old favorites" of the 1930s and '40s. This Elderhostel class is entitled "Boogie, Big Band Blues & Bop" and is sponsored by the University of Maryland Eastern Shore. Fran Mahr has been introduced and waits next to bill for her cue. The sheet music is on a stand in front of her.

A beautiful woman, Fran looks theatrical, dressed all in black: narrow pants, turtleneck sweater and a long, sleeveless jacket. A black, satin, brocaded scarf, with a tinge of bronze color in a raised pattern of roses, is draped loosely around her neck. Silver and onyx earrings set off the outfit and complement her silver hair.

Frances Mahr, nee Schleider, has been singing since she was 3 or 4 years old. At her mother's urging, she often performed for guests in their home. On special occasions, her mother, Bess Schleider, always did two things: set out a table of sweets and insisted that her daughter sing. Later, Fran studied at the Peabody Conservatory of Music, in Baltimore, and as a teen-ager she performed in musicals at the Hilltop Straw Hat Summer Theatre, working with such show-biz biggies as Alice Ghostley and producer George Shaeffer.

Throughout the early years of her life, she had been groomed to pursue a career in musical theater, to go off to New York to seek success. But, in 1951, at age 18, love prevailed and she married Malcolm Mahr, a handsome, established businessman, whom her parents also adored. That, however, was not the end of her singing career, and Fran now says, "I probably did more singing and acting in Baltimore and Washington than I ever would have in New York." She sang in nightclubs, acted on

The Singer

stage and did radio and television commercials. She has sung with such greats as jazz pianist Ray Bryant, who became a close friend and who still comes to Maryland to work with her.

Fran feels that she is now entering a second phase of her career, which may keep her even busier than the first one. Her performance with Bill Messenger and Elderhostel is, as she sees it, just uncovering the tip of the retirement-age audience. People her age and older not only enjoy hearing an experienced singer, but they also identify with one who has lived through the same decades, danced to the same music and remember, with fondness, the words of the same songs.

As Fran begins to sing, a warm smile stretches across her face, her eyes shine, and her hands reach out in gestures of friendship to the Elderhostel students. But it's her voice that pulls them in. A woman who had been knitting looks up, her hands now still. A man who had been taking notes from Bill's lecture stops and leans forward; his foot begins to tap in time to the music. Heads move, lips silently mouth the words and smiles become uniformly wide.

Fran's voice has matured with the mellowness of a fine wine — deeper, richer, softer — blended with phrasing that makes familiar words and music seem new. What her voice does for a song is what hot fudge does to ice cream. It can slide lightly over an upbeat version of "I'm Old Fashioned" and then melt you as it caresses "As Time Goes By."

The latter song, Bill Messenger explains, was written in 1931 by Herman Hupfeld, and was a flop until it was rediscovered in 1942 and used for the movie "Casablanca." Hupfeld became a one-hit songwriter, but the royalties from that one song were enough to keep the composer in comfort, as all the rest of his time went by.

And Bill gets a laugh when he relates how the composer of another old hit, "Ain't She Sweet," went back to his hometown and was confronted by his English teacher. "Didn't I teach you that ain't isn't good grammar?" she asked. "Yes," he replied, "but it's great money."

Many of Bill's extensive repertoire of anecdotes about composers and performers have been provided by the relatives and friends of those celebrities during countless interviews that Bill has conducted.

"'Showboat,'" he explains, would probably have been forgotten, rather than repeatedly revived, if it hadn't been for its most popular song, which wasn't part of the original score. Producer Flo Ziegfeld had run out of money and had to delay the show's opening. During the interim, Oscar Hammerstein wrote a new lyric, but his collaborator, Jerome Kern, didn't want to write any more music for the show. "The score's finished," he said emphatically. So when Hammerstein insisted that it be added to the show, Kern took it so lightly that he sat at the piano and simply reversed the opening notes of another melody in the show, the "Cotton Blossom" theme. But those throw-away notes became the beginning of "Old Man River." Then Bill cracks up everybody by telling them how angry Hammerstein's widow would become whenever anybody talked about Jerome Kern's "Old Man River." "Jerome Kern didn't write 'Old Man River,'" she would snap, "my husband did. All Jerome Kern wrote was dum-dum-dum-dum," sounding the monotonic opening notes.

Bill also explains musical origins. For example, jazz was originally called "spasm music," because that's the effect it had on many listeners. One of the most popular bands in New Orleans of the late 1800s was the "Razzy Dazzy Spasm Band." That would be a great name for any of the new bands that are reviving what our grandchildren call swing dancing, but which we called jitterbugging. Incidentally, Bill Messenger says the origin of the term boogie woogie may be the Bantu phrase "Mbuki Mvuki," which means "I take off in flight," which is a pretty good description of the music and the jitterbugging it inspires.

The Singer

The Elderhostel students, informally called Hostelers, applaud with energetic enthusiasm at the end of the presentation. Then they rush to share their own stories with Bill Messenger and to compliment Fran. Jack and I take the opportunity to find out what has attracted these people to Elderhostel. The reasons are as numerous as the students in the class. Everyone at this session has attended other Elderhostel programs — the more they've attended, the bigger the bragging rights. "I've been to 14," one woman says. "That's nothing," respond a husband and wife, "this is our 40th." One woman tells us that she first heard of the program when she was vacationing in Homer, Alaska, with her daughter and there was a sign in the lobby of the hotel, "Welcome Elderhostel." Her daughter suggested that she should look into it and now, the woman says, "It's the only way I vacation." She adds, "It's a safe way for singles to travel."

There are also many love stories — single men and women who have met at Elderhostel events, fallen in love and married. Many such couples continue taking Elderhostel trips, booking double occupancy.

Marie and Walter Bartnick, from Long Island, N.Y., signed up for this program in Ocean City because they are scouting the area for a possible move. Their daughter lives in Laurel, Md., their son in Reston, Va. They'd like to move closer to them, but they want to live near a beach. Several months earlier, they attended an Elderhostel program sponsored by the Delaware Technical and Community College, which housed them at the Sands Hotel on the Rehoboth Beach boardwalk.

Elderhostels can be found up and down the Delmarva Peninsula, from the Delaware Bay to Assateague and Chincoteague. The Marine Science Consortium/Wallops Island Marine Science Center conducts at least a dozen courses, from "Barrier Island Botany" and "Birding on Virginia's Eastern Shore" to "Waterfowl Management." One woman said, "I hope I live long enough to attend all the Elderhostels I've circled in my catalog — and don't run out of money to do them."

There is one charge for residential attendance at each of them. It includes housing, three meals a day and the fees for the courses of that program. However, people who live close enough to commute can pay a significantly smaller amount to just take the classes and some of the meals.

Libraries have Elderhostel catalogs and information on the programs: national, international, intergenerational (programs you can attend with a grandchild or a young companion) and the volunteer service program, which is like an Elderhostel Peace Corps.

On a cold, windy night, the Elderhostel classes at Dunes Manor end on a warm note, as Bill Messenger performs as if he is George Gershwin, taking on the composer's character, to relate Gershwin's life and his music.

Sitting at the grand piano in the hotel lobby, surrounded by the students he's worked with for the past week, Messenger-turned-Gershwin talks of brother Ira Gershwin, calling him, "The smart brother." (I guess even geniuses have smart brothers.) Ira Gershwin was more serious and studious than George and became one of the world's most acclaimed lyricists, working with other composers after George's death.

We listen to selections from "Lady Be Good," the first complete show George and Ira wrote together. Ira also improved the titles of George's wordless compositions, for example, changing "Rhapsody in Blues" by simply dropping the s.

Between renditions of "American in Paris" and other favorites, we also hear about Ethel Zimmerman, a big-voiced singer trying out for a Gershwin show, who was looking for a better stage name. The name Zim was offered and so was Zimmer, but finally between the singer and the composer it was decided she should shorten her last name by using just the last two syllables — Merman.

After a Bill Messenger arrangement, in which the lyrics describe Gershwin as "S'wonderful and s'marvelous," he stands up, takes a bow, and says, "It's been a good week — good night." We all applaud our agreement.

Chapter 20

Beach Watch

Winter, so busy in other parts of the country this year, waits until early March to book a brief stay at the beach. Spring flowers, snow drops and crocuses are already blooming and daffodils budding when the more seasonal cold weather moves in. The flowers close up, along with schools, as four to five inches of snow accumulate throughout much of the area.

Then, another storm brings heavy rain and a strong wind out of the northeast, plastering the dune grass flat and whipping stinging sheets of sand across the beach. Even Angel is ready to go back inside after only a few minutes.

The few people who brave the storm walk backward on the beach, against the strength of the blasts. But the wind does smooth the beach, filling in holes and blowing sand through the slatted snow fencing to build up the size of the dunes.

Throughout the night, rain and wind pound the beach house. I lay awake listening to the wind whistling around the windows and rattling the panes. The huge beams holding the structure together groan loudly, as if warning that even they can take only so much.

"The wolf's still out there huffing and puffing," Jack says following a fitful sleep, "and this house isn't made of bricks." "No," I agree, "it's made of sticks and built on sand." "So what are we doing here?" Jack asks with a nervous laugh.

Beach Watch

As former television reporters, we have both witnessed the devastation caused by severe storms, and we have a healthy respect for them. But along with volcanoes, earthquakes and tornadoes, powerful storms are fascinating to watch.

When you live at the edge of an ocean, you can be lulled into a false sense of security. Few things are as soothing as the sight and sound of lapping waves. But even at their gentlest, the waves are constantly changing the shape and size of the beach. And once you've heard the ocean roar during a storm that rips away 15 to 20 feet of beach in a single day, you become acutely aware that your life, in that beach house, rests only on a temporary foundation and that some day the ocean will take it. It can make you wonder, as you watch the ocean, whether the ocean is also watching you.

Although storms are the biggest threat to beach communities, ironically, it was a storm that transformed Ocean City, Md., from a small fishing village, into the major beach resort it is today. That storm, in 1933, is described as a "100-year storm," which refers to its unusual strength and intensity, not its frequency, because such storms can happen at any time. That storm tore away an entire section of the island, separating Ocean City from Assateague and creating an inlet between them.

Realizing the potential of the inlet, Ocean City preserved it by installing a stone groin and creating a channel, which then attracted more fishing boats, more people, more money and more growth. It also helped create Ocean City's famous beach, which was made much wider, near the jetty and the boardwalk, because those same stone groins have blocked the natural movement of the sand that would have migrated to Assateague Island. Since then, Assateague has receded significantly.

But the bigger beach gave Ocean City a false sense of security, encouraging the construction of buildings on the beach, so that when a similar storm swept through in 1962, many of the buildings were destroyed, along with the boardwalk. The beach, most of which was deposited on Coastal Highway, had to be trucked back to its original location, and supplemented with sand from Assawoman Bay.

In South Bethany, Del., all the homes built on the dune line, about a half-dozen in all, were destroyed by the 1962 storm. However, construction along most of the Delaware beach communities has been done much more responsibly than in South Bethany or Ocean City. With few exceptions, the oceanfront homes, such as the one we're living in, have been built behind the protective dune line.

Even so, in storms such as the one in 1962, which everyone around here still talks about, the dunes offer only partial protection as waves wash over and around them and often tear them away. We're told that the house next to "ours" was relocated by that storm. It was lifted up off its foundation by the waves, moved back and turned 180 degrees to the right. The front porch, which had faced the ocean, now faced a side street. The owners, perhaps feeling that Mother Nature is the ultimate architect, left it that way.

And Silver Lake, the fresh-water lake that is separated from the ocean by several hundred feet of sand and dunes, was also flooded with saltwater during that same storm.

Beaches move. Despite man's best efforts to stop them, beaches are moved constantly by wind, waves and currents. And there is continuing debate about the cost to taxpayers in trying to maintain the beaches at ocean resorts. It has become increasingly expensive, especially where the resort communities have allowed homes, hotels and condominiums to be built so close to the water that the dune line, a beach's natural protective barrier, has been destroyed. Many believe that with beach repair projects and federal flood insurance, such property owners are being unfairly subsidized with tax *dollars that could be used elsewhere. The cost of constructing a man-made replacement dune line in Ocean City was more than $60 million.*

In the past, erecting sea walls to stop the ocean from taking beachfront buildings and extending stone jetties into the water in an attempt to stop the ocean from taking sand from the beaches produced mixed results. But now, a more effective and much more expensive process, beach replenishment — the pumping of sand from the ocean floor onto the beaches — is being used extensively in America, Europe and elsewhere.

With the ocean perilously close to beachfront property, Ocean City and the Delaware resorts began beach replenishment in 1988. Some warned that throwing a lot of new sand at a beach and hoping that most of it sticks would only stick the taxpayers with another vain attempt to fight the natural forces of nature.

In preparing a television series on the Maryland/ Delaware beach project, I interviewed Orrin Pilkey, a marine geologist at Duke University and recognized as the foremost authority on beach dynamics. He supervised a study of replenished beaches along the East Coast.

"All of those beaches," Pilkey said, "all of them, with one exception, were washed away within five years, most within two years."

The one exception was Miami Beach, which had much smaller waves than the other beaches and also had not been hit by a major storm. Nevertheless, Pilkey said that though replenishment was only a temporary solution, it was the best solution available, short of more drastic action. "If I were king of Ocean City," he said, "I'd not hesitate to remove the buildings next to the shoreline."

"Just knock them down?" I asked.

"Knock them down, yes. That's the only way the island can be preserved. But," he added, smiling resignedly, "I'm not king, so don't worry about it."

Some resort communities in North Carolina have moved cottages off their beaches. But in Maryland and Delaware the buildings are too big and too numerous. Anthony Pratt, Environmental Program Manager for the Delaware Department of Natural Resources and Environmental Control, says that if Delaware were to buy the 65 homes on South Bethany's shoreline and remove them, it would cost tens of millions of dollars, and the gain would only be an additional beach width of 50 or 60 feet. Beach replenishment, Pratt says, is the only option, and the commitment to renourish or resand the beach every two to four years is a relatively minor cost for Delaware — an average of a million to a million-and-a-half dollars a year. Meanwhile, Congress has approved funding for the federal share of such maintenance, to avoid paying much more for storm damage to homes and property that are declared disaster areas after a big storm.

Nancy Howard, who headed Maryland's Beach Replenishment Project, said, "Consider this atoning for our sins, if you will. We've made mistakes in the past, and now we're paying for them, literally. And what we're doing is trying to give the beach back." And it has worked, with development beyond the dunes now restricted.

The replenishment project has also become a tourist attraction. Special boats, anchored offshore, dredge up tons of ocean bottom sand, which is then pumped through pipelines and spewed out, in huge, arcing gusts, onto the shore, where bulldozers spread the new sand and shape the expanded beach.

The beach is not only Anthony (Tony to his friends) Pratt's profession, but it's his passion as well. Like many of us who grew up in the Baltimore area, a summer without going to the beach didn't seem like summer at all. When he was growing up, Tony says he spent every summer of his life on the beach in Ocean City.

As a teen-ager, he worked at a stand renting beach chairs and umbrel-

Beach Watch

las at 14th Street. He learned to surf, relishing the power of the ocean in his endless search for the perfect wave to provide the perfect ride. On his surfboard, he experienced how waves roll and curl on their crash course with the shore. He observed back then something that helps him understand what he's dealing with now, that all waves come in at an angle, moving sand up and down the beach. "Try counting the waves one day," he said to Jack and me, while visiting us at the beach house.

I did. Approximately nine per minute or roughly 13,000 a day crashing onto the beach, which explains why the beach moves so much.

In January, we experience what seems like a minor storm, a small nor'easter, but one that hits during the high tide of a full moon. Meteorologists refer to this as a spring tide, when the tide, as well as the moon, is at its fullest each month, and not just during the months of spring. Tremendous breakers pound the beach, sending spindrift back across the next line of waves rolling in close behind. The wide, foamy edge of the ocean swirls close to the snow fencing around the dunes.

When the storm passes and the ocean recedes, we see that a large chunk of beach has been torn away, leaving a steep cliff mid-beach. Along the entire length of the shore, tons of replenished sand have been reclaimed by the ocean. But later, we see that the sand hasn't gone very far. It is deposited offshore, as a sandbar that wasn't there before.

We observe in the weeks following the storm that what Tony told us would happen is happening. The sand cliffs that the storms create, especially where replenished sand has made the beach deeper, are reconfigured into a gradual slope to the water. Wind and waves cause the cliffs to collapse, and the waves bring back the sand from the sand bars, which have been built up, or inflated, as Tony describes it, near the breakers.

These sandbars, often visible at low tide, are created by the waves during the ocean's high energy periods. This usually happens, although not always, during winter, and then more often than not the sand is redeposited in summer, when wider beaches are more necessary to accommodate the tourists. It is further proof, if needed, that nature can also be kind and accommodating.

Beach Watch

Tony, among others, insists that maintaining beaches is essential. "Try to imagine life without beaches," he says. "How do you estimate the cost of that?" And the cost of maintaining beaches, he argues, is a bargain compared with the cost of maintaining man-made resources, such as roads and bridges, many of which have been built for the express purpose of getting people to the beaches.

"Does it make sense," he asks, "to build two parallel Bay Bridges, the tunnel, the Kent Narrows bridge, a new Wilmington bypass route to the beach and all the other projects — costing hundreds of millions of dollars, and then not maintain the beach that is the destination of those projects?" Tony estimates that yearly maintenance for just the new bypass — such as grass cutting and repaving — will probably exceed the annual cost of maintaining the Delaware beaches.

To extend life and to improve or maintain its quality, most of us invest in preventive maintenance, not just for our homes and cars, but also for ourselves: visits to doctors and dentists, medicines, skin care, exercise, proper diet, hair care, clothes. Why should we not do the same for such natural resources as beaches that also contribute much to our quality of life?

Delmarva officials also note that the maintenance costs are more than offset by tourist and tax revenue. The philosophy "life is a beach" is espoused by millions of day-trippers, weekenders and weekly or monthly renters, not just beach home owners.

As he is leaving, Tony sums up his thoughts. "We have found ways to prolong life and improve its quality — environmental life, as well as human life — how foolish it would be not to take advantage of what we've learned."

I find myself thinking about that comment as I walk the beach with Angel on the first really warm day of the week before spring. The tide is at its lowest, exposing the expansive sandbar that the winter waves have left us. Angel is playing in a tidal pool that has formed between

the beach and the sandbar. The sun is bright, the breeze gentle. I feel
the rejuvenation of the season, as replenished as the beach, and certain that our off-season time here has added much to my life.

I will turn 60 in the upcoming summer, an age that now seems
much younger than it did before. My grandparents on my mother's
side died in their early 60s. Jack's mother's parents died in their 50s.

Most of us are now living longer, healthier lives. Tony Pratt is right:
to ignore what we've learned, to miss a day such as this, even if it
saves us money, would be to waste the gift of life as we can have it
today.

*The beauty and tranquility of the beach nourish the
mind and the senses. The healthfulness I feel extends
beyond the merely physical.*

Chapter 21

Cape May/
Lewes

The mid-morning, midweek ferry to Cape May, N.J., pulls out of the Lewes Terminal precisely at 10:20, right on time, in its off-season schedule. Fewer than two dozen vehicles have boarded the ferry, and they are lined up close together near the front exit. The rear of the ferryboat is empty. It's been several years since Jack and I last visited Cape May and three decades since I last spent a summer vacation there with my children and their father, my first husband. We stayed with his family, who had a summer home there. Cape May was the first beach experience my children had, although there was relatively little beach there at the time.

The 1962 storm that extensively damaged the Maryland/Delaware shoreline hit Cape May especially hard, ripping away almost all the beach north of the boardwalk and taking the boardwalk as well. Later, a huge rock and concrete seawall was constructed where the beach and most of the boardwalk had been. Only a limited section of boardwalk was replaced — in front of the beach pavilion and the resort's relatively small seaside commercial center.

Beyond that, extending north and south, a macadam promenade was created on top of the seawall. The promenade had to be crossed to reach the ocean and the beach that was left. However, my children loved it.

The memories bring smiles: my young children playing on the beach and in the water during the heat of August and then, as we headed home, all three of them squealing with exaggerated suffering while high-stepping across the hot macadam surface in their bare feet, racing to the lighter-colored and cooler concrete edge — and me, their young mother, suppressing a smile and scolding, "I told you to put on your sandals."

Occasionally at dawn, my son, Jody, and I would ride our bikes to the south end of Cape May to watch the sunrise and have breakfast at The Cove restaurant. Then we'd race back down the promenade to get back to the cottage before the others awoke. I explained in my book about Jody's life and death, "Everything To Live For," that was just one example of the time we created to be together, to nourish the special bond we both felt.

My two daughters, Marjorie and O'Donnell, were aged 6 and 4 years old, respectively, when the 1962 storm hit, so they have only vague memories of playing on Cape May's formerly wide beach. But their memories of what it was like after the storm are vivid — sunbathing on the rocks and climbing down to swim in the ocean. At low tide, the girls and their brother, Jody, along with their cousins, played in the small semicircles of beach where the rocks of the seawall and the stone jetties connected.

Eventually, the Cottager's Association bought the property where most of the remaining sand was, and built a beach club. We were members, and although the children then had a large beach to play on, they found it less satisfying, because it could only be reached by car.

Standing at the railing of the ferryboat, with my memories, I look out across the sun-dappled Delaware Bay and listen to the drone of the engine and feel its vibrations. A seagull races alongside, easily pulling ahead of the 5,000-ton boat, which labors along at 12 knots. The captain had announced that the trip would take 75 minutes, plenty of time to think and reflect.

When Jack and I last visited Cape May, I was astounded by the changes. What I had known as a sleepy, rather sedate and weathered beach community had undergone a complete make-over. Many of the large Victorian houses, built as single-family summer cottages, that showed age and neglect during our family visits, had been renovated, brightly painted and turned into bed and breakfast inns. Entire streets had been transformed. The houses of brown shingle and white clapboard were now wearing every color of the rainbow and were being referred to as Cape May's "Painted Ladies." The famous Victorian "gin-

gerbread" now scrolled across porches and outlined roofs in shades of pink, purple and orange. And Washington Street had been closed off to create a pedestrian mall with shops and outdoor cafes.

On that summer weekend several years ago, when Jack and I arrived in Cape May without reservations, the town was jammed with people. It took hours of searching before we found one room available, and that only because of a last-minute cancellation. It was at the King's Cottage, an inn just a short walk from the still lovely south beach. Our room cost $180, but some of the room rentals in those refurbished homes were as high as $300 a night — and probably more by now. The husband and wife who owned the King's Cottage were friendly and accommodating, our stay a pleasant memory.

That evening, we savored the best margaritas we've ever had as we relaxed on the porch of the Virginia Hotel on Jackson Street. A young woman tending bar there made the drinks from scratch. (We hope that, if she's not still there, they're at least still using her recipe.) We also had a delicious meal in the hotel's dining room.

Jack and I walked the streets of Cape May, stopping in several of the restored homes and admiring the changes. As we walked, we paused frequently to absorb the imaginative color combinations on the houses and in the gardens.

The abundance of flowers was breathtaking — in little front gardens, over gateway trellises and window boxes. It was Jack's first visit to Cape May, and he was enchanted by it.

Now, the ferry taking us on our winter trip to Cape May is halfway across the bay, and I find myself wondering what changes we will find this time, actually hoping things will be the same, and thinking about lunch at the Virginia Hotel, with a margarita first to renourish that remembrance.

We move around to the starboard side of the boat, where the sun is warm and there's protection from the strong northwest wind. The historic lighthouse at Cape May Point comes into view. My booklet on Cape May/Lewes tells me that this lighthouse was built in 1859, but that it's the third such structure on the Point. The first was built in 1823. The booklet doesn't tell me what happened to that lighthouse or the second one, built in 1847. But, for 176 years now, a lighthouse has served as a continuous warning and navigational guide at that point. The light flashes every 15 seconds, and can be seen 24 miles out to sea.

My earliest lighthouse memories come from the days that my children and I went out to the Point to look for Cape May diamonds. These are small, white, almost translucent stones that wash up on the beach at the Point. They're so smooth and shiny that people often make jewelry out of them. I've never seen them on other beaches, in Cape May or elsewhere.

"Where do you want to go first?" Jack asks as we leave the ferry and drive over the bridge spanning the Cape May Canal. "To the right," I say quickly, "Let's go down to the south end of the beach. I want to see if that restaurant I used to go to with Jody is still there." It's there and still called The Cove, but it's closed, the first disappointment on our off-season trip to Cape May.

> *For me, the biggest disappointment is the oceanfront — now tinged with tackiness. The charm of the big, old hotels, some gone, others in disrepair, are overshadowed by motels and storefronts, none of which fit into any of my memories.*

The one exciting discovery and biggest change — the beach. Thanks to an extensive beach replenishment project that included building sand dunes up against the full length of the seawall and pumping tons of sand, the beaches, north as well as south, are once again wide and white.

I can't believe what I'm seeing. We drive north and park on Queen Street, the same street I had walked across 35 years ago with three little children in tow to sit on the rocks.

I race, with camera in hand, up onto one of the widest beaches I've ever seen. I want to capture this on film for Marjorie and O'Donnell or they'll never believe it either. But when I cross the beach to the edge of the ocean, so that the photograph will show the full breadth of the beach in the foreground, the familiar houses along Beach Drive look so small I'm afraid my daughters won't recognize them. I snap the photo anyway, it's so impressive. The beach that vanished one stormy night when they were young is back. While I'm running around being amazed and taking pictures, Jack spots two young women tossing shells.

Although they are laughing, they are obviously involved in some sort of intense competition. These two young women are playing a game with seashells that neither Susan nor I had ever seen during our decades of beach experiences. The women explain that it's a variation of horseshoes, but not played with horseshoe crab shells; they are using clam shells. "It's called clamshoes," one of the women explains, "at least that's what our dad called it. He taught it to us when we were kids. He learned it when he was a kid and spent the summers in Cape May, working in the bakery up on the boardwalk."

To play clamshoes, you first dig a small hole in the sand and then draw a couple of circles around it. About 12 to 15 feet away, you draw a line in the sand, from which you toss the clam shells at the hole. You get the most points — 10 — if your shell lands in the hole, similar to a ringer in horseshoes. You score two points for every shell that lands in the smaller, inner circle and one point for the shells that land in the larger outer circle. The player who scores 50 points first wins. Try it with your grandchildren; there's nothing to buy, it's fun and it may delay their pleas for more boardwalk time.

Cape May's rebuilt beach has led to a boom in new homes — or perhaps sand castles might be more accurate. At the north end of the resort, huge houses — Jack calls them faux Victorian — are being erected all the way up to the formerly isolated Cottagers Beach Club.

The resort of Cape May, dating back to the 1700s and considered the first seaside resort in the United States, has undergone several periods of rebirth. It has survived war and fire as well as storms. Long popular with vacationers from Philadelphia, Cape May began attracting rich plantation owners from the Tidewater regions of Maryland, Virginia and the Carolinas in the 1800s. Huge hotels were built. The largest, the Mt. Vernon, could accommodate 3,000 guests and could serve 2,000 people in the dining room at one time.

Cape May's economy suffered a devastating blow during the divisiveness of the Civil War, but the resort was revived in 1863 with the rail line that brought northern industrialists to enjoy the seashore offerings. Then, just 15 years later, in 1878, a tragic fire destroyed 30 blocks of the city. Rebuilding and another period of rebirth continued into the 20th century.

Throughout its history, Cape May has attracted people who fall in love with its location and charm, providing a way of life and contentment they've not found anywhere else.

Andy O'Sullivan, an architect from Flemington, N.J., vacationed here as a child with his family. And now he and his wife, Carrie, own and operate The Victorian Lace Inn, at the corner of Stockton and Jefferson streets. The inn is the centerpiece of their retirement dream. Their five children are grown, and now Carrie lives in Cape May full-time, while Andy commutes, weekly, to continue his design/build business in Flemington. But in several years, Andy, who is in his late 50s, will stop commuting and do design work at their Cape May inn, letting his son take control of the business in Flemington.

As with many couples, retirement for the O'Sullivans means continuing to do work they love, in a place where they love living, which for this husband and wife is Cape May. Carrie enjoys the cultural offerings, such as the arts center and the endless activities that are staged year-round. Cape May does not close down completely in the off-season, as it once did. That's the reason the O'Sullivans keep their inn open all year. They've added fireplaces, so that every suite has one, and converted the original ones to gas for safety reasons. Unlike some inns, children are welcome here. "We have rules," says Carrie with a laugh, "and the kids have to follow the rules. But I love having them around."

I smile, thinking about all the children who ran through that same house in the '60s — three of them mine. You see, the O'Sullivan's inn, The Victorian Lace, was once the beach house of my first husband's family. It is the heart of all the memories I have of Cape May.

The house looks so different now, with three apartments. Back then, it was a big, old-fashioned single-family house with eight bedrooms. On summer weekends, all the bedrooms were filled. Yet, though the house has changed, much is the same: the big porch where we gathered on hot summer evenings and inside, the center-hall staircase. I can still see my children and their cousins, who were supposed to be in bed, sitting on the landing of that staircase to observe the adult parties, where we'd sing around the piano and dance in the large living room. My former mother-in-law, Willie White Hechter, loved to entertain, and no one in Cape May threw a better party than she did.

Jack and I vow to spend a night here on our next trip. We realize with this day trip, that an off-season visit to Cape May needs the guidance of a year-round resident, such as Carrie O'Sullivan.

Crossing the Delaware Bay by ferry to visit Cape May, or Lewes, if you're coming from Cape May, is a pleasant trip any time of year. However, as a result of our March visit, we found that the winter months may not be best and not just because of the weather. It can be more costly, and fewer of the attractions are open.

The ferryboat fares are $2 less, but because there is no shuttle bus service at the terminals in either Cape May or Lewes during January, February or March, you almost have to take your vehicle with you, ruling out the much cheaper foot passenger fare of $4.50 one way, or $8.50 roundtrip. For us, it cost $22.50 each way. Trolley/shuttle bus service, available daily during the summer, is also available on weekends in the spring and fall. I'm told that weekends in December are wonderful in Cape May, with all the Victorian Christmas decorations and the numerous events and activities that are held for the holidays.

The ferry also has a much lower fare for bicyclists. So bicycling to and from the ferry terminals is an option, if you like bicycle rides of several miles. But walking, unless you're a distance hiker, is out of the

Cape May / Lewes

question. If you don't have someone to meet the ferry, drive you around and take you back to the ferry terminal, rule out traveling as a walk-on passenger in the winter months.

In March, we find there are more places getting ready to open than those that are open. The Virginia Hotel is not serving lunch, only dinner, and we can't find out if the hotel still makes those wonderful margaritas because the bar is closed until evening. We find only two restaurants on the Washington Street Mall open. The one we try leaves us full, but not impressed. Or as Jack phrased it, "appeased our hunger, but not our expectations."

Driving out past Cape May's charming marina and commercial fishing dock, known as Fisherman's Wharf, we realize we should have gone to The Lobster House, which has a long-standing reputation for good food and is open year-round.

There is a variety of shopping in Cape May and Lewes. Again, not all stores are open, but enough to be tempting. I've found Lewes, with many up-scale, imaginative stores, a great place to browse and window shop. In one shop window, I saw a colorful silk blouse with a tropical fish pattern. I thought it would be perfect for my "Bermuda Collection," the clothes I buy, save and only wear once a year when we go to that island. I take the same clothes year after year, occasionally adding something that seems appropriate, such as that blouse in the Lewes shop window. However, the $235 price tag attached to it nixed its entry into my less extravagant island wardrobe.

In Cape May, there are souvenir shops as well as boutiques on the Washington Mall. You'll find T-shirts and sweatshirts with Cape May emblazoned across them, along with handmade sweaters. There are also several candy shops with assorted confections that can be shipped or eaten as you stroll, as Jack does.

We leave on the last ferry of the day, which, during off-season, is 5 p.m. It's the same in both Cape May and Lewes. The setting sun creates a path of gold, as if leading us back across the bay. We sail with old memories and new ones.

Chapter 22

The**Artist**

One of my longtime friends, Kitty Roberts, who is Weeder's mother, moved to the Eastern Shore of Virginia — many miles from her Baltimore roots and even farther from the lifestyle we shared as young wives and mothers. She lives independently now in a cottage overlooking Church Creek, pursuing her lifelong passion to paint.

At 64, Kitty is still shapely and pretty. The bounce in her step still causes her soft, almost shoulder-length, highlighted brown hair to swing about in the same sassy, youthful way. On a cool March day, when Jack and I visit her, she hurries out of the front door to greet us, bounding across the porch in jeans and a pastel-colored cotton sweater. Her bare feet sport bright, luminously blue nail polish.

Inside, a fire in the wood stove, with a book and her reading glasses on the chair beside the stove, paint a picture of how she had been before we arrived.

Kitty moved to Franktown, Va., with her second husband. When they divorced, she went back to using Roberts, the last name of her first husband, with his permission and that of his wife, Phyllis, whom Kitty calls her wife-in-law. Wanting to stay in Virginia, Kitty moved into this cottage, which is on the property she shared with her second husband. Kitty now owns the house and several acres that surround it.

She has spent three years restoring the 200-year-old house, uncovering the innate beauty that had survived, despite years of

The Artist

neglect, and that has been enhanced now by the artistry of Kitty's talent and commitment.

Like many small clapboard colonials of the 1700s, Kitty's cottage was built in sections. Over the years, as families needed them or could afford them, new sections would be added. Thus, her house evolved into what it is today — three room-sized rectangles, butted together, end to end. On the first floor is a small foyer and staircase, powder room, living room, kitchen and dining room. But with no central hallway to connect them, you must pass from one room to the next.

Upstairs is her master bedroom, a large bath and a smaller bedroom that she's decorated for her granddaughters, Posey and Marley.

The single-story dining room, the original section of the house, doubles as a studio where Kitty does her watercolor painting. The room has windows on three sides, providing northern light from the modern addition of large arched panes in the pitch of the roof. The exposures from the east and west come from the traditional windows on the front and back walls.

Outside, Kitty has painted the original clapboard siding and the wooden shutters a country yellow; the windows and trim are white. The painted surfaces are thickly textured from the centuries of accumulated coats of paint. "Covering this with vinyl would be a sin," Kitty says of the "quick fix" way of redoing an old house. A jasmine vine, trained on a trellis, runs over the doorways and windows along the front of the house.

The back porch extends around the side of the cottage, where a grouping of white wicker furniture waits for warmer days. Between the chairs, a glass-top table encases a collection of beautiful feathers: peacock, yellow song bird, wild turkey, barn owl, a sand hill crane and many others.

Inside, Kitty did all the painting and wallpapering, made slipcovers and curtains and refinished the floors. The walls of each room are adorned with original art, some hers, but mostly other artists she admires. Each room has a large window view of the expanse of lawn and gardens that lead to a cliff and a boat dock, all framed by the waters and shoreline of Church Creek. The dock was badly in need of repair when the property became hers. "It cost me $3,500 to have that repaired," Kitty now says. "Fixing that, I couldn't do myself. Just think how many clothes that money would buy — or the eye lift or tummy tuck I could have gotten," she says, and laughs at the missed opportunities.

Kitty Roberts, who was a working mother with a busy social life that included elegant dinner parties and country clubs, has learned a new way of life, one she prefers. "It's the freedom and simplicity of things down here. People are warm and friendly, but not intrusive," she says with quiet reflection. But she admits it took some adjustment. When a friend expressed shock that Kitty had never been fishing, Kitty wisecracked, "So, I bet you've never been to a cotillion." They both laughed, and with her new friends she has learned to fish and to explore the waters and shores of the bay. And by going across the peninsula, just about 10 miles, she has experienced the exhilaration of an undeveloped Atlantic coastline and the natural state of Virginia's barrier islands not far offshore.

The Eastern Shore would never be called cosmopolitan. The closest thing here to a sushi bar is a bait shop.

Ignore him! To appreciate the offerings of Virginia's Eastern Shore — the quaint villages and towns, the stately farms, colonial mansions and watery vistas — one must get off Route 13, with its clutter, billboards and strip shopping centers. One attraction along the highway toward Kitty's house that she advised us to stop and see is the Turner Sculpture and Art Gallery. "People come from throughout the country to see it," she said.

We did stop, and it is impressive. Turner Sculpture is advertised as the largest privately owned and operated bronze foundry and gallery in the United States. The extensiveness of the operation and the art collection housed within could never be anticipated by what you see from the road. As soon as you enter, you know you're not in some souvenir shop. The life-sized bronze statue, near the door, is a young boy poised to swing a baseball bat. The first copy of this statue was bought for the home of Baltimore baseball great Cal Ripken Jr.

The Turner bronzes carry price tags ranging from hundreds to hundreds of thousands of dollars and are in museums, universities and private homes.

The man behind Turner Sculpture, the artist and founder, is Dr. William H. Turner, a former dentist. Bill Turner, 64, is a Clint Eastwood

The Artist

type: craggy faced, tall, thin, quiet. A man apparently absorbed by his creative instincts, or perhaps just shy upon first meeting.

He is a man who grew out of his modest rural roots, profiting from the richness of nature all around him on Virginia's Eastern Shore — marshes, bay, ocean, islands and farms.

From boyhood, he was fascinated by all the creatures that inhabited his homeland. He has written about them in his books, and he has sketched and painted them. But mostly he has sculpted them. They surround him in bronze — wild ducks and geese, deer, herons, life-sized and miniatures — every imaginable animal, bird, fish and reptile, so beautifully crafted they look as if the real thing has been dipped in bronze. A pig stands out back, as if waiting to go to market, but it's simply being readied for the gallery.

There are also aquatic displays, life beneath the sea, captured in bronze.

I wander off to look more closely at the several rooms of art that Turner and one of his three sons, Dave, have created. There are also numerous newspaper stories about them, along with letters from such notable patrons as former President George Bush and Barbara Bush praising the work. When Bill and Susan catch up with me, he says his assistants are about to pour some bronze and asks if we're interested in seeing it. We are.

He leads us to the foundry, where three men are putting on protective clothing, similar to the space suits worn by astronauts. From an oven, they slide out a cart filled with white molds of assorted creatures and pieces of creatures that have been sculpted in clay. The men then lift a large kettle of molten bronze, heated to nearly 2,000 degrees, and begin pouring it into the molds. Bill shows us similar castings that have cooled and demonstrates how easily the white covering brakes away, revealing the beautifully detailed bronze figures.

As he shows us the rest of the complex, we see numerous sculptures and paintings, not yet finished, revealing Bill's seemingly ceaseless urge to create. He explains that he had turned over his dental practice to his son, Bill, several years ago so that he could devote full time to what he loved the most, art — making his hobby his career.

It had begun, he said, with whittling wooden figures as a young boy and, through trial and error, he taught himself to do sculptures. Being paid for doing what you love to do is everyone's dream. Bill Turner is living his dream. "And," he says with a wry smile, "it pays better than dentistry."

And a lot better than writing, but Bill Turner hints that the time is coming when he wants to spend more time on his farm, writing, fishing and just enjoying the wildlife, instead of using them as models for his art.

Bill Turner is one of the many people here on the Virginia shore who has befriended Kitty. They are people whose families have long been rooted in this remote, rural part of the Delmarva. "There are 'came here' residents and 'came from' natives," Kitty says without resentment, "I'm clearly a 'came here,' but they've never treated me as an outsider, never."

Another of her friends is Suzanne Wescoat, a woman in her late 50s who decided, in 1985, to plant a vineyard. From her first planting of 1,000 cabernet vines on an acre and a half, Suzanne has steadily increased the vineyard. The vines of merlot, chardonnay and cabernet sauvignon now twist across 20 acres, on row after row of neat, perfectly straight trellises, and are carefully pruned by Suzanne and one full-time employee.

Suzanne's husband, Jack, is an attorney in Eastville. They both grew up on the Eastern Shore of Virginia, and he was the first boy she dated. His parents drove them on that first date. Suzanne and Jack have two children, a boy and a girl, and now two grandchildren.

Suzanne says, with a distinct Southern accent, "When our children became teen-agers, I wanted to try something on my own. I had been a teacher; I didn't want to go back to that."

Suzanne says that one day, in a doctor's office, she saw an article in a woman's magazine about being happy. It listed four things that make most people happy. She can still quote them from memory:

The Artist

"1. Spiritual Belief. 2. Meaningful Relationship. 3. Job Fulfillment. 4. Try Something New." She decided then and there to try something new. "I love being outdoors. I'd seen vineyards in Europe. A few were cropping up in Virginia. We had the land — I don't know — I'm the kind of person who just jumps into something and says 'which way is the current going?' I had no earthly idea how to begin — I just did it." And she has done it successfully. She sells her grapes to a winery in Williamsburg, which has designated her chardonnay grapes for separate bottling; they are that good.

Perhaps fueled by her accomplishments in the vineyard and a deep-seated sense of civic responsibility, in 1995, Suzanne Wescoat ran for public office and was elected to the Northampton County Board of Supervisors. Earlier, she had started a group called Citizens for a Better Eastern Shore.

She says of her community involvement, "Virginia's Eastern Shore is on the brink of tremendous change. We who live here must be involved in helping to create our own destiny and not just let whatever happens happen."

For a woman who says that she once drifted with the tide, Suzanne Wescoat now seems to have channeled her life with definite purpose, understanding her priorities, which she lists without hesitation: "1. Family — grandchildren. 2. Expanding the vineyard. 3. Helping to shape the future of the Eastern Shore."

Of her busy life, she says, "I used to be a fantastic cook, and I'm sure my husband wishes I still had time to do that. But I guess I take after my mother, needing to try new things, trying to keep life fresh and interesting. My mother is 86," Suzanne continues proudly, "and she just got a computer. She says she wants to see what this e-mail and Internet is all about before she has to leave this world."

Kitty Roberts has many such friends, but, most importantly, she has also learned to live comfortably with herself. "I watch the sun rise out that way," she says, pointing toward a window, before turning and pointing to the windows on the opposite wall. "And then I have the beautiful sunsets over here. To be able to see them both gives you an enormous feeling about just one day. Each beginning and ending is so spectacularly different that it gives you a sense of the importance of just one day, not just in nature, but in a lifetime. That's why I try to paint every day, to do something with my art each day. I don't know," she pauses with her thought, "I just want to learn to be really good at something, at this age, at this time in my life."

"You are good," I say, not trying to flatter her.

"I'm getting there," she says, "I know it's in me. I just have to get it out."

Kitty is currently working with watercolor. A collection of her paintings, stacked on a dining room chair, displays the range of her talent. There are houses, landscapes and still lifes, including a room of furniture in various shades of just one color. Jack is taken with a painting of cabbages. Kitty laughs. "I did that one in class," she says, as if it should only be considered as an exercise.

The class she is taking is being given in Cape Charles, the tip of the Virginia peninsula — a 20-minute drive from Kitty's home. She takes us on a tour and points out the old school building that now serves as the new art center. Driving through the town, we see newly renovated houses, a new upscale restaurant and improvements to the dunes, all signs that Cape Charles is undergoing a kind of rediscovery.

> *Cape Charles, the southernmost community on the Delmarva peninsula, borders the Chesapeake Bay and was once a vital hub for steamship, ferry and rail traffic. But after World War II, all that changed, as most of Cape Charles' population moved away. Now, however, it is clearly in the midst of a renaissance. Homes there are being sold as quickly as they go on the market. Aging and abandoned late Victorians are being treated to face-lifts by new suitors, who want a weekend getaway. The buyers are coming from as far as Baltimore, and of course, from Norfolk and other Virginia cities, by way of the Chesapeake tunnel. A new industrial park will also provide many new jobs for permanent residents.*
>
> *With plans for two golf courses, one designed by Jack Nicklaus and the varied activities provided by its location on the Bay, Cape Charles is hoping to have everything in place for the next generation of retirees, the baby-boomers.*

Another new facet of Kitty's life on the shore is that of a hospice worker. "I took the training and I volunteer. But," she adds quickly, "it's as much for me as for them."

"Why?" Jack asks.

"Because I had this huge family and nobody said to me, 'Aunt Elizabeth's dying, come sit with her, talk to her, give her hugs, tell her it's OK.' All the older people in my family are gone — my mother, my father — everyone and I didn't get to do that with any of them. So now I do it for other people's families — and for me. It's helping to repair that huge hole that was left when the older generation of my family was all gone. And it's helping me to face the fact that I'm that older generation now — the next generation to die.

"I went to a wedding recently, and all the young people in my family — nieces and nephews — had little children or were pregnant. It was wonderful, really reassuring — all those bright, happy kids are going to replace me." Kitty pauses, not because talking about this makes her uncomfortable, but to reflect on the importance of what she has learned about life and death. "Funerals are big down here — I mean, really big. Everybody goes to a funeral. People take off from work; they take time off from everything, but they go. When people care that much about a death, it lets you know how much they care about a life."

Although clearly comfortable with her own mortality, Kitty Roberts is planning to live at least until she's 80, but accepts that life will be different for her then. "I have the dress I'm going to wear when I get old," she says, "perhaps on my 80th birthday — or maybe I'll get it out for your 75th, whichever comes first." she says to me, with the same devilish lilt that's been in her voice since she was a girl.

"What do you mean you have a dress to wear when you're old? Why do you have it now?" I ask, not knowing what to expect from my unpredictable friend. "I got it for the rehearsal dinner before Weeder's wedding. She insisted that I wear this dress or one like it. You know how I like dresses up to here?" Kitty points mid-thigh. "And cut down to here?" she points mid-breasts. "Well, my daughter said, 'Just this once, Mom, I want you to wear a proper dress.'"

At my urging, Kitty and I race upstairs, like schoolgirls, so she can dig out the dress, from in back of the closet, to show me. Jack trails behind us shaking his head. It is an expensive dress of gold silk, with a pattern of tangerine-colored roses and aqua flowers of some sort; it has fussy shoulder flaps and the wrap across the front pulls up in gathers. But the length is below the knee, and the neckline would reveal little or no cleavage. It also has a solid beige satin slip, which resembles a long undershirt.

"Did you wear it?" I ask, giggling at the image of Kitty in this dress.

"Of course, I did. Weeder said I had to. And I'm going to wear it again — when I'm old."

"When you're 80?" I ask.

"Right!" she says, "I'll wear this dress and start smoking again when I'm 80."

"Why start smoking again?" Jack asks.

"Why not?" Kitty replies, "at 80, whatever time I have left I'm going to spend doing everything I can that makes me feel good — especially in that dress."

Chapter 23

Spring

The headline of a small item in the local paper catches Jack's eye: "Wanted: beach gardeners." It's an appeal for volunteers to plant dune grass along several miles of the Delaware coast at Dewey Beach. We sign up. On the morning of the planting, as we fortify ourselves with a substantial breakfast at the Sunrise restaurant, I find myself thinking about how much a part of this community I now feel. Everything is so familiar and comfortable. We have been here almost exactly six months; our allotted time is just about up. We have done so much, and yet there have been many days of doing almost nothing but simply enjoying — especially you-know-who. But today Jack is in high gear, looking forward to participating in this project. And so, a few minutes past 9 a.m., we join the other volunteers at the designated beach starting point at the end of Dagsworthy Street.

One of the volunteers, a gray-haired man, shouts to a nearby group of teen-agers. "Last year, when we did this, everyone was wearing shorts." The man laughs, but the teen-agers can only manage wan smiles. They are cold, despite their heavy coats and hats pulled down over their ears. Nevertheless, they keep working — planting beach grass in the new sand dunes that bulldozers had recently created along Dewey Beach.

Spring

According to the calendar, it is now spring, March 27, but few days of the recent winter have been colder or more blustery. At least the rain and snow that the weather forecasters predicted hasn't materialized.

Susan and I are among the approximately 200 people who have signed up for the annual Beach Grass Planting, organized by Delaware's Soil and Water Conservation Division. Sand dunes help protect the beach and homes against damaging costal storms. But it is the beach grass, which grows long and tenacious roots, that holds the dunes together and helps the dunes grow by trapping wind-blown sand as it passes over the grass. It is easy to understand that process, because a lot of wind-blown sand is being trapped in our hair, ears and clothing as we plant the grass. Later, we shake enough of it loose to help replenish the beach in front of our cottage.

Team leaders hand out bundles of beach grass culms, or stems, along with pointed sticks, each with eight-inch-long blue tips to measure how deep the grass should be planted and a 24-inch red strip at the other end to measure the distance between each planting. Susan, however, digging to the beat of a different drummer, uses a gnarled piece of cedar driftwood. She says it makes her feel more attuned with the beach, even though I point out that it makes her grass plantings more out of sync with the depth and distance of my plantings.

Several volunteers are from Pittsburgh. They explain that the shortest distance between them and the ocean is the road to the Delaware seashore — about a six-hour drive. Every year, they commit to planting grass, to help the beach they think of as theirs. But, among the volunteers, teen-agers greatly outnumber adults, which, we've observed, is usually the case with similar civic projects. Such young people seldom make the news, but they make us feel confident about the future. Working side by side with them, enjoying their infectious laugh-

Spring

ter and enthusiasm, is one of the most satisfying things we have done here — all of us helping to give something to the beach, which has given so much to us.

The line of dunes that has been designated for planting stretches beyond where our beach house is located. Unfortunately, the planting doesn't get that far. As a result of the unpleasant weather, not as many volunteers have shown up as had been expected. However, Jack asks for two bundles of grass to take with us, so he can plant them on the dune in front of "our" cottage. We hope the owners will be pleased. We owe them so much.

A few days earlier, just as I was thinking our stay was near the end, they called from California. "We're not coming back until June. If you'd like to rent the house for two more months, you can."

Our hearts overrule our budget. Two more months, April and May, warm months. We will experience the entire off-season at the shore, going home Memorial Day weekend, just as the summer crowds begin to arrive.

I tell my daughter, Marjorie, "We just can't pass up this chance — it's too good an offer to turn down." "Don't feel guilty," she says, laughing at my trying to justify taking this additional time away from the duties at home. "I don't," I say, meaning it. "Your time will come, Marjorie, and when it does, I hope you'll make the most of it, too."

So many more sunrises, never the same way. One morning, the sun suddenly bursts from the sea, so red it seems angry. But, the next morning, as it slowly emerges from the fog, it looks completely white and cool, like the moon. And on the following dawn, the sun begins as a pale pink crescent rising out of a slate blue haze, its color slowly intensifying as it becomes fully formed.

I've come to think of this period in our lives as the "carefree days," the time between taking care of and, possibly, being cared for. Our children are on their own, our parents are gone; who knows how much time we have before someone needs to take care of us or one of us will need to care for the other? Time is running out for second chances. Opportunities no longer have to be missed or sidetracked because of career or even family.

And so we extend our stay. We'll get to see the wisteria bloom on the trellis over the front door. The flowering tree beside the house is already in bud. From beneath the winter-worn clumps of dried goldenrod, new green shoots will emerge in pursuit of the next season's gold. And the dune grass will turn green; the new stalks Jack and I planted will grow.

Perhaps the children and grandchildren will come back. We'll play clamshoes on the beach. Jay turns 14 in May. Maybe he'll come down to celebrate. Maybe his dad will come with him to surf. Maybe all the boys can come back. Even if it rains, there's always the Yo-Yo Man. Emily, who turned 16 in March, will be getting her driver's license; maybe she and a girlfriend can drive down. It could be a good experience, if her parents agree to it.

Or maybe we'll just selfishly savor this time on our own. We've already moved down into the big, second-floor bedroom with the four-poster bed. Our guests have enjoyed its luxury. Now we will.

Our writing will be finished, at least on this book. Jack may be getting back to "our" novel, his book, screenplay or TV script, but I'm going to sit in the sun. And I'm going to go on a diet, so that my southern exposure fits into my summer clothes. I've already tried out a new exercise for Angel and me — bicycling on the beach at low tide. There is a wonderful wide stretch of hard-packed sand, left by the winter waves. I pedal and Angel runs alongside. So, she stays trim as I begin to get fit.

At the very beginning of our off-season stay in this beach house, when the thrill was new and emotions high, Jack said, "If you could, would you want to buy this house?" Without hesitation I said, "No!" If I could afford to buy this beach house, or one like it, I could afford to go anywhere in the world, experience other lifestyles, get to know other areas and people of the United States or foreign countries. And maybe we can do that, even without being rich.

March 30. The sun is warm on the front porch as we share our morning coffee. The forecast says it will be a 70-degree day, and instead of packing to leave, we are settling in for another two months. "Sometimes you don't have to be a millionaire to live like one, do you?" Jack says, still amazed by our good fortune. "Would you like to do this again?" he says, "if it's offered?"

"You bet," I say, "but remember there's a lot of world out there. How about the coast of Spain during its off-season," I suggest.

"Or Italy or Greece," Jack replies.

"Or California," I add, thinking of Christopher. We laugh and sip our coffee, as we shift our gaze to the now-familiar view of sky, ocean and beach — both of us entertaining the possibility of such far-away vistas becoming just as familiar as this one.

When I was young, these weren't the kinds of plans I thought people our age would be making. I suppose because our parents didn't. Growing old scared me, but my son sees what we're doing, and he's really looking forward to doing the same thing. Only, of course, he says he'll do it sooner and better.

Stay tuned!

Epilogue

Post**scripts**

Letter from beach house guests:
"The Raynor Travel Guide has rated the White-Bowden 'Elderhostel' a five star establishment. Accolades go to the crab soup, Swiss cheese omelets, the ocean view from the celestial bed and the friendly support staff, 'Guardian Angel.' The educational seminars of critiquing movies, as well as the political discussions, media updates and a variety of other subjects apropos of almost nothing will prove invaluable."

Marjorie & Charlie Raynor

April 14, from Susan's notebook:
Extending our stay has its moments of melancholy. Ever since my son's suicide in spring 1977, I've felt the need to be close to home this time of year.

The April before his death, I took several days away from my job at the TV station to spend them in Annapolis with Jack, while he covered the last days of the legislative session. It coincided with Jody's spring break from school, and I wanted him to go with me, "sort of a

Postscripts

mini-vacation," I told him. He begged to stay home. Things weren't going well with his girlfriend, and he wanted to stay close to her. It turned out to be a traumatic period in my son's life. When I got back, his romantic relationship and, it seemed, his world, had crumbled, and I hadn't been there to help or comfort.

Now, 23 years later, the uneasy regrets still haunt me, my impulse to stay home now an attempt to erase the guilt. I guess I still believe that if I'd been home then I could have, somehow, secured a future for my son. Experiencing the death of a child is never a matter of "getting over it;" it's a matter of "going on." Knowing that helps. And as I walk the beach with Angel this April, I make a conscious effort to think of the joy Jody and I shared at the seashore, in Cape May and in Ocean City, when we had that gift of time.

April 24 weekend:
Christopher and Melissa come back to the beach to say goodbye. Christopher has gotten the job he wanted with an Internet company in San Francisco. He's excited about the move and the opportunity. Melissa will eventually join him there. We sit in the sun, talking endlessly, walk the beach and enjoy two spectacular meals (dinner and brunch) at The Back Porch restaurant. The parting is hard, especially for Jack. The separation will be an adjustment. We will have to find a way to stay close — frequent phone calls and visits. Christopher gives us his old computer. We'll learn how to use it and get into e-mail. Perhaps our next extended trip will be to California.

May 2
For three days, a harsh wind out of the northeast has pounded the Delaware shore — no rain, just a steady, powerful wind caused by a storm off the coast of North Carolina and more unrelenting than any storm during the winter. It churns the surf and tears at the beach. The house is built to give, but there is a groaning of its timbers, and the

windows vibrate with what sounds like howls of protest.

Nevertheless, for the first two days, the sky is clear and bright, a brilliant sun seeming incongruous with the other sights and sounds related to the wind, as if disconnected from the weather system causing such fury. Sheltered from the wind, the temperatures are spring-like, mid-70s. We make use of the sun porch carved into the rooftop. It faces south, and the walls provide total protection from the north wind, while giving full exposure to the warmth of the sun. As the coast is pounded and weekenders who brave the beach bundle up, I bake in the sun, achieving a head start on a summer tan and finishing a good book — "Bella Tuscany" by Frances Mayes, who wrote about her six-month stay in Italy. Now, I really, really want to do the same thing.

May 4
Our first dolphin sighting of the spring. Their shiny, dark backs arching gracefully above the surface, just beyond the breakers is a seasonal sign — nature's balance of constancy within periods of change.

May 6
>*One change for me, near the end of our stay, is I can no longer run. Running is great exercise, but too hard on my body. I quit running once before, when my right hip became so sore that even walking was painful. Eventually, by doing leg presses, the pain disappeared. But when similar pain hit my left hip while running along the beach this spring, I quit for good. There are plenty of other aerobic exercises. I swim more now, and when Angel and I venture out to see the seagulls, we walk instead of run.*
>
>*Every morning, the seagulls gather at the same spot on the beach, much like the groups of elderly men*

who meet at the same shopping mall bench every day. There is a St. Lawrence street sign adjacent to the gulls' gathering spot, and I can't help wondering if it's the gulls' signpost, as well as the residents'. Dozens of seagulls stand together on the beach, all facing the same direction, as if listening to something we humans can't hear. As Angel and I approach, they suddenly stir, fluttering up, over and around us — like a scene from "The Birds" — but then quickly settle back in exactly the same spot. If we then cross the beach alongside the nestling gulls, they remain grounded, only sidling a few steps away as we pass.

May 13

On the calendar for this day: Golf lesson with Steve Smith, the pro at the new Golf Park on Country Club Road. I'm determined to learn to play at this late stage in my life. Jack is determined to play without saying those words he also uses when someone shrinks his favorite sweater.

Everyone we asked in the Rehoboth area recommended Steve Smith. They are right — he's good. Steve knows just what to say and when. And he's entertaining. He works on Jack's Civil War swing ("Shoot and fall back") which is a factor in his tendency to slice. With both of us, Steve stresses the basics — grip, stance and, most of all, balance. As Jack's shots sail down the middle, he says, "Why didn't I take these lessons years ago?" and I wonder why I've waited so long to learn. Steve has me hitting the ball smoothly the first time out.

"It's all in the grip, positioning of the body to the ball and the follow-through swing, a 'Hollywood finish,'" according to Steve. Even if the ball doesn't go very far, your swing looks good. "Don't worry about long," Steve says to me, "just worry about balance." If I can learn to play well enough to play with my grandsons, I'll be happy. Steve Smith says, "No problem."

May 17

We pack up, clean with extra care, say goodbye to all we've come to love, put Angel in the car and depart. It is time, and we are ready. The crowds are beginning to return, and there is lots to do at home.

May 21

Jack leaves for San Francisco to help settle Christopher into his new apartment and to settle his own apprehensions about his son being 3,000 miles away.

> *Even before my son left for San Francisco, Susan had begun insisting that I visit him there. But I insisted it was best to just let him get on with his life and career, without his father looking over his shoulder. And it was best for me to get used to his being so far away. But when Christopher called and asked me to come, I immediately made reservations.*
>
> *San Francisco: He is happy to have company; Melissa is still working in Philadelphia and won't join him for another month. It will also be that long before their furniture arrives, so we sleep on the floor, using inflatable mattresses.*
>
> *I haven't been to San Francisco in more than 20 years, so while Christopher works during the day, I get reacquainted with what, to me, is the most beautiful city in America.*
>
> *It is perfect, except for one thing, which I quickly realize on my first full day of walking the streets of San Francisco — Susan isn't here to share it with me. I miss her terribly. I call her from a pay phone, not wanting to wait until I get back to my son's apartment, and tell her that from now on we will travel everywhere together. She agrees. I'm surprised to hear that she misses me, too — she's still brainwashed after all these years.*

Postscripts

Christopher and I share meals, lift weights together, go touring on weekends and talk about everything.

We even see the new "Star Wars" movie together, just as we had shared the earlier ones, when he was a young boy. Unfortunately, we both hate this one.

Susan laughs, and is genuinely pleased, when I tell her that my former wife, Christopher's mother, has arrived in San Francisco for a weekend visit — staying with her sister, Barbara Davies, who helped raise Christopher. My former wife's name is also Susan — Susan Bowden, having kept my surname, which has created some confusion and many jokes. We have remained friendly, and when I married Susan (confusing isn't it?), she happily attended our wedding. She, too, liked our son's new stepmother. And the biggest laugh of that day came when the former wife caught the new wife's bouquet.

Christopher's enthusiasm for his new life is infectious and reassuring. California is now his home, and for me it no longer seems so far away. The visit has given me a new serenity about my son, as Susan, the wise and loving stepmother, knew it would.

When Christopher takes me to the airport, we hug and chat briefly. Then, as I turn away to get my luggage, I hear my son say, "I love you, Dad." This is not the first time he's told me that, but as he's grown older, the occasions are rare and now usually it is hurried, sometimes mumbled and in response to my saying, "I love you."

This time, it is neither hurried nor mumbled and without any prompting. It takes me a moment to respond, needing to swallow the lump in my throat, "I love you, too," I say, both of us smiling comfortably.

Just before my father went into surgery for a risky operation, I had told him that I loved him — probably for the first time since my childhood. Not many men said that to each other, not even fathers and sons. The look in my father's eyes and on his face as he reached out to touch my face and say, "I love you, too," is one of my most vivid and cherished memories. He died a few days later.

I know he would be pleased that my son didn't wait so long.

June 9th:

A long time ago, when the grandchildren were very small and promises for the future easy to make, costing nothing, Jack and I made a pact with them that, the year they turned 16, we would take them to Bermuda to see what we love so much about that island. In March of this year, our oldest, Emily, came of Bermuda age. Believing promises should never be broken, if at all possible, and truly wanting to share Bermuda with the children, off we go for five glorious days. Thank goodness for credit; it can make promises come true. The trip is everything we hoped it would be and much, much more.

My goal, when I first got the idea, was to open up a different world to our grandchildren at the impressionable age of 16 — a world away from the daily routine of family, school, friends, sports and the limitations of any one place. It works. Emily's eyes are opened, and so are ours, re-experiencing the excitement of discovery through her. We take in our surroundings, almost as if it's the first time we've seen the aqua water and pink sand, white-roofed pastel cottages, limestone cliffs, hedges of hibiscus and morning glories, pink and white oleander, as profuse as they've ever been. We absorb this exquisite world and sample as many of its pleasures as possible in the five days.

We ride the mopeds, reminding ourselves each time to "Stay left — stay left!" They drive on the "wrong" side of the road here. We explore the beautiful beaches on the south shore and swim with the dolphins of Dolphin Quest at the Southampton Princess beach area. We ride the ferry into Hamilton to shop. And we talk, as adults, as friends.

One woman at the hotel where we are staying comments on how well we and "our daughter" seem to enjoy each other's company.

"Granddaughter," I correct.

"Oh," she says, seeming relieved, "that explains it."

Postscripts

"Yes," I say laughing, "the secret to traveling with a teen-ager is to skip a generation."

To me, Emily is more than my granddaughter — in a way, I think of her as a daughter. When Susan and I married, we tried to have a child, but it was not to be. A couple of years ago, Susan said to me, "Do you realize that if we'd had that child, he or she would now be a teen-ager that we couldn't send home? Would you be up to that at your age?" I had to admit we were probably better off. However, having thoroughly enjoyed raising my son, I'd long wondered what it would be like to have a daughter. Emily has provided, at least in part, that experience. Bermuda brings us even closer.

On June 10, while we are in Bermuda, Jack and I celebrate our 20th wedding anniversary. It is all the more special having Emily here with us.

In two years, our three middle grandsons will all turn 16, and we're planning to take all of them together. We'll see if our philosophy, credit cards and Bermuda hold up to the test of our "grand" plan in triplicate.

With three boys, there will, unfortunately, be less opportunity for one-on-one conversations. But we'll play golf together. And when one of them slices his ball, as I often do, then I'll be able to talk with him, one-on-one, as we walk through the rough together, searching for our errant shots. Plus, it will give me an alibi: "I only hit the ball over there so I could talk to the boy."

Aug. 3 — Return to Delaware

The colorful crowds of summer have claimed the miles of vacant sand we called ours during the off-season. Umbrellas, beach chairs, towels, surfboards and bodies, with varying degrees of sunburn, stretch out along the coastline. The crowds grow with the heat of the day, across the width of the replenished beach. The sociable settings of children and adults cover the sand from the breaking waves to the wavering dune grass, in its first season of growth. It seems to me that Jack's planting in front of the beach house has taken superior root.

It's the day before my 60th birthday. We've come back to celebrate and to finally meet our beach house benefactors, Judi and Phil, and their children. When we see them on the beach, we recognize them instantly from the photographs that kept us company throughout the fall, winter and spring.

> *Judi, holding their newly adopted fourth child and first boy, named Jack, jumps up, and uses her free arm to give each of us a hug. Phil says, "We feel like we already know you, from those wonderful notes and photographs Susan sent us."*
>
> *"We feel the same way about you," I say, as we shake hands.*
>
> *Judi holds out the baby to me and says, "Jack you want to hold Jack?" It's been a long time since I've held an infant, but little Jack is comfortable and so am I.*

Judi and Phil had previously adopted three girls and had wanted another girl, but when they were offered this newborn boy, they didn't hesitate. Their birth announcement reads: "The Sorority Has Gone Coed! Proud sisters Erin, Christy & Isabelle welcome Jack Phillip; 6 pounds, 6 ounces; 19 3/4 inches." Already, the baby seems comfortable on the beach, in the shade of the umbrella, now tucked securely back in his mother's arms.

Our friends, Weeder and Andy Obrecht, join us on the beach with their daughters, Posey and Marley. They've just returned from several weeks in Nantucket.

"How was it?" we ask.

"OK," Weeder replies, "But I like Dewey Beach much better than Nantucket."

"Why?"

"Here, I'm one of the Beautiful People," she laughs, and so do we,

Postscripts

knowing how she feels.

During this visit, Jack, Angel and I are staying at the Silver Lake Inn. We're in one of the apartments where, as co-owner Mark (the man with the tennis racquet) told me, they allow dogs. It's after 5:30 p.m., so Angel is also on the beach meeting "the family."

Four-year-old Christy falls in love with Angel. Judi says that Christy had been intrigued and excited all winter that a dog named Angel was living in their beach house.

Down by the water's edge, I teach Christy how to make Angel sit, then stay, before throwing the tennis ball for her to retrieve. Christy goes through the routine tirelessly, and Angel gets used to the erratic and unpredictable direction the ball takes from the little girl's hand.

They bond.

Marley, who's 4, digs in the sand, while 8-year-old Posey joins Judi and Phil's eldest, 7-year-old Erin, in the ocean. They swim the waves with the experience and confidence that comes with being much older than the other girls. However, 2-year-old Isabelle, with long blond hair, big blue eyes and bright orange floaties on each arm, catches the attention of the beach assemblage, all of whom smile as she determinedly totters toward the ocean as if driven by some genetic instinct.

We quickly feel like old friends of this family, whose beach house we shared, and as close as family to the Obrechts, who brought us together. At dinner with them at Fusion, one of our favorite Rehoboth restaurants (there are many), Jack expresses our gratitude. "We want to thank you for making possible the best year of our lives." He is right. That is not in the least an overstatement, fawning or excessive. It is factual, and we all feel it's truth.

The next day, I experience the best birthday I've ever had. The one I wasn't looking forward to, the one that seems different somehow, sounds so much older than all the rest. Sixty years old is more than half-way, no matter how farsighted or optimistic you are.

But it is the best birthday ever. Shortly after the allowed time, we bring Angel out on the beach to join us, and we stay until dark. Jack gets carry-out from Jake's seafood restaurant — a clambake without the work. The Obrechts bring us a chilled bottle of chardonnay. The Obrecht girls walk their dogs. Judi and the baby come to sit with us awhile. (Phil has gone back to California for a few days on business, so we didn't get to visit with him as much as we'd have liked.)

Isabelle again comes out with her floaties on and immediately heads for the water. She frolics in the shallow waves, with Angel hovering over her, staying with Isabelle the entire time she is rolling around in the waves, seemingly ready to grab the child if she goes under.

With the setting sun comes the mellow light that wraps up a beach day in a patina of gold. The color washes over the sand and tints the white-edged waves. A warm, mellow hue to reflect our contentment.

As we raise our glasses in a toast, the crystal catches the sun's slanting light, adding new dimensions to the wine's rich color, which seems, somehow, symbolic of the changes within us.

The glow of sunset fades, giving way to the peace of darkness, which carries in its starlight embrace the promise of a new day just beyond the horizon.

Each day is unique — in nature and in life, regardless of age.

Postscripts

Favorite restaurants

Our favorite restaurants in the Dewey-Rehoboth Beach area are listed here, in order of preference in each category. However, from our own experience, and that of many residents, the quality and ranking of restaurants in the expensive category, may vary significantly from season to season, or even month to month. Off-season schedules also vary radically from year-to-year.

Expensive . . .
Fusion
Back Porch Cafe — *Closed most of the off-season*
Blue Moon
Garden Gourmet
Espuma on First at Wilmington — *Opened the spring of 1999 and quickly became a favorite*
The Buttery (Lewes)
Chez La Mer — *Closed most of the off-season, but we're told is a favorite in-season with established long time residents and vacationers.*

Moderate . . .
The Big Fish
Yum Yum Pan-Asian

Rusty Rudder
Rose & Crown (Lewes)

Best Value . . .
Sunrise — *Breakfast and lunch only*
Great American Diner
La Rosa Negra Italian (Lewes)
The Crystal — *Rehoboth Ave. near Route 1. Local favorite. Closes at 3 p.m. off-season.*

Best Beach Food Carry-Out . . .
Sunrise
Sharkey's Grill — *Best crab cake sandwich and best conversation while waiting for order, with Sharkey himself. Closed November through March.*

Favorite Pizza . . .
Nicola

Thanks

To . . . Charlotte Kurst, the first to read a partial draft of this manuscript, who gave us her enthusiastic encouragement to complete the book, and asked if her husband could read it, published or not.

Special thanks to . . . Deborah Golumbek, SunSource general manager, who, at 30-something, "got it," "loved it" and knew immediately that she wanted to publish it. Her calm, effective control in the final push to deliver on deadline qualifies her for a job in broadcast news, or a hospital delivery room. Though it would be publishing's loss.

Thanks to . . . Editor Melinda Greenberg, of the same youthful generation, who found time in her busy "prime-time" life, as a magazine editor, wife and mother of two young boys, to become involved in our Off**Season**.

And to the entire creative SunSource production staff, who met last-minute changes and challenges, our gratitude: Laura Gamble, sales and marketing manager; Jennifer Halbert, design; Cari Pierce, marketing; and Ray Frager, copy editor.

And to . . . All who shared their stories and our Off**Season** experience, most of whom are named in the contents of the book. But also to all who are not, such as Jay Windsor, the resident plant authority in Rehoboth Beach, who identified the bushes in front of the beach house, that I was incorrectly calling Carolina Jasmine, as "elaeagnus pungens." And Chester (Chet) Stachecki of the Delaware Department of Natural Resources/Fish and Wildlife who explained the workings of Gordons Pond and talked at length about sharing nature with his grandchildren. We had a lovely conversation.

Everyone we met in Rehoboth, Dewey, Lewes and up and down the shore was wonderful, gracious, kind and helpful. We came to love you all — and we'll be returning again and again, usually in the Off**Season**.

About the authors

Susan and Jack were both born in Baltimore and educated in Maryland. Jack's broadcast career spanned more than 40 years beginning at WMUC, the campus radio station of the University of Maryland, College Park. He went on to work at WFMD in Frederick, WBAL and WMAR in Baltimore and WJLA in Washington, D.C.

Susan began her professional career as a free-lance model, in television and magazine ads, before moving into television news. Upon joining WMAR, in 1967, Susan became the first woman on-air reporter to be hired by the news department of that station.

The Bowdens live on the family farm in Finksburg, Maryland, when they're not traveling somewhere — living the dream.